PERSONAL MEMOIRS OF U.S. GRANT

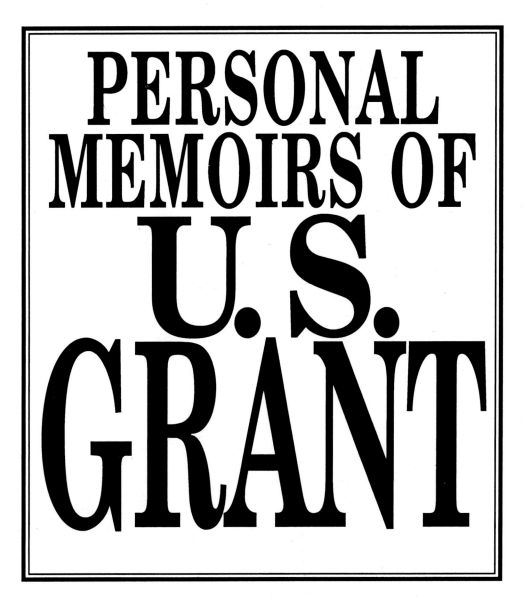

PERSONAL MEMOIRS OF U.S. GRANT

Crescent Books

New York/Avenel, New Jersey

PAGE 1: Grant and his staff in
1864. On the far right is
Grant's secretary, Ely Parker.

PAGE 2: Ulysses S. Grant.

THIS PAGE: City Point, Va., one
of Grant's main supply bases
in the 1864-65 campaign.

CONTENTS

This 1995 edition published by Crescent Books,
distributed by Random House Value Publishing, Inc.,
40 Engelhard Avenue,
Avenel, New Jersey 07001

Random House
New York · Toronto · London · Sydney · Auckland

Produced by Brompton Books Corporaiton,
15 Sherwood Place,
Greenwich, CT 06830

ISBN 0-517-14002-0

8 7 6 5 4 3 2 1

Printed and bound in Hong Kong

Editor's Preface

Overwhelmed by debt, former-President Ulysses S. Grant in 1884 belatedly set about writing his memoirs in the hope that the resulting royalties might in some measure help to provide for his family. He had hardly begun when the task took on a new urgency: in the autumn of that year his doctors informed him that he had an inoperable cancer and had only a little while left to live.

Beset by mounting pain and physical exhaustion, Grant struggled on with the manuscript for the remainder of 1884 and into the spring of 1885. By this time he had not even the strength to work at his desk and was obliged to write on a pad held on his lap while he sat propped up in bed or in an easy chair. Plainly his race against mortality would be a near-run thing, but in the end, as he had once so often done on the battlefield, Grant gained the victory. He died on July 23, but he had completed the last chapter of his manuscript a few days earlier.

Titled *Personal Memoirs of U.S. Grant*, the two-volume work was published later that year by Charles L. Webster & Company, a publishing house partly owned by Grant's good friend Mark Twain. The book was an immediate success, selling some 300,000 copies and netting his widow the then-impressive sum of $450,000. But it was not long before the work was recognized as something a good deal more than a commercial blockbuster. The way we view it today is well summarized by *The Columbia Encyclopedia* when it says, "Solid and unpolished as Grant himself, these memoirs rank among the great military narratives of history."

Military the memoirs assuredly are. They cover only the first 43 years of Grant's life (ending with the Grand Review of the victorious Union armies held in Washington in 1865), and less than 10 percent of the original 1216-page printed text deals with matters not directly concerned with the Mexican or Civil wars. But whether the *Memoirs* deserve to be called "unpolished" is at least debatable. Grant's style is certainly plain and direct, but it admirably expresses the author's personality. The narration on the other hand, is exceptionally skillful: fast-paced, colorful, leavened with pungently-expressed opinions, and adroit in its blending of significant detail and historical sweep. At times the reader might wish that Grant would go a little farther in analyzing the quality and significance of some of his battlefield achievements, but it is also clear that for him to have done so would have been inconsistent with his essentially modest personality. In any case, it is not really necessary: the achievements speak for themselves, and there has never been any want of able military historians ready to draw instructive comparisons between Grant's generalship and that of Napoleon or Alexander.

This illustrated edition of the *Memoirs* has been abridged to cover the most significant episodes of Grant's service in the Civil War. Details of his life before 1862 are summarized in the introduction that follows this preface. The remainder of the text consists of extended excerpts from the *Memoirs*, these being linked where necessary by short bridging passages supplied by the editor. Cuts in Grant's original text that do not require editorial bridges are indicated in the conventional manner, *ie.*, by ellipses consisting of three or four periods or, where there is a change of subject, asterisks.

The only other liberty taken with Grant's text has to do with proper names. Grant adheres to a time-honored military prose tradition by omitting the first names of a good many of his fellow officers, a convention that civilian readers may sometimes find confusing or irritating. In this edition the editor has attempted to supply as many missing first names – or at least initials – as he was able, always indicating the interpolations by enclosing them in brackets.

Finally, the many captioned maps and illustrations that embellish this new edition of the *Memoirs* were of course not present in the 1885 edition. The current editor and publisher can only hope that General Grant would have approved of them.

BELOW: The house in Detroit, Michigan, in which the newly-married Ulysses and Julia Grant lived during 1849-50 while Grant was still serving in the peacetime army. After Grant's death in 1885 local veterans bought the house and decorated it (as shown here) as a memorial to their great Civil War commander.

OPPOSITE: A portrait, with scenes of Grant's life. The scenes show, clockwise from the top left, Fort Donelson, Shiloh, Vicksburg, Missionary Ridge, Grant's elevation to lieutenant generalcy, Lee's surrender, Grant's West Point graduation, Chapultepec (in fact San Cosme), and Grant drilling the 21st Illinois.

Introduction

The man whom history knows as Ulysses Simpson Grant — greatest Union general of the Civil War and 18th President of the United States — was born Hiram Ulysses Grant. The date was April 27, 1822, and the place was a two-room frame house in Mount Pleasant, a little Ohio River town that had sprung up on what was then still very much the American frontier.

"My family," Grant wrote proudly in the opening sentence of his *Memoirs*, "is American, and has been for generations, in all its branches, direct and collateral." True enough, the first American Grant had settled in New England just ten years after the Pilgrims landed at Plymouth, and the Simpsons (Grant's mother's family) had been farmers in Pennsylvania since the

LEFT: Formal portraits of Grant, such as this one, show us his features but usually fail to convey the "rough and ready" style that was both a feature of his personality and a hallmark of his method of command in the field.

OPPOSITE TOP: Julia Dent Grant, as she appeared in the 1870s when she was First Lady.

OPPOSITE BOTTOM: Frederick Tracy Dent, Julia's brother, had been Grant's roommate at West Point. He would serve as one of Grant's aides-de-camp in 1864-65.

late 1730s. By the early nineteenth century, as the young United States began to expand westward, contingents from both families gravitated towards the frontier, and that was how 27-year-old Jesse R. Grant came to meet and fall in love with 23-year-old Hannah Simpson in Mount Pleasant at a time when the State of Ohio was itself less than 20 years old. The couple married in June 1821, and Hiram, the first of their six children, was born the following spring. In the fall of 1823, when Hiram was one, the family moved to a larger house in Georgetown, a county seat a little to the east of Mount Pleasant. This was where Hiram would spend his next 16 years.

Jesse Grant was a tanner by trade, and a moderately successful one. Orphaned when he was 11, he had been obliged not only to make his own way in the world but to be primarily responsible for his own education. As a result of this early conditioning he was both a very determined, hard-working man and a voracious reader. He never questioned that young Hiram should be exposed to the best formal schooling the region had to offer.

This, alas, was no better than it should have been, and in his *Memoirs* Grant is somewhat dismissive of his early education (as, indeed, he is of his life in Georgetown generally). The highest branches of learning he was ever taught, he says, were "Reading, 'Riting, and 'Rithmetic," and he claims that he had been made to repeat "A noun is the name of a thing" so often "that I had come to believe it." Yet whatever its shortcomings, his early schooling would ultimately prove good enough to get him past the rigorous West Point entrance exam without much trouble.

Hiram was never a particularly social boy — not shy, but reserved and somewhat withdrawn. He loved animals of all sorts and was uncannily good in dealing with them: he was an expert horseman virtually from the time he could climb into a saddle. One consequence of his devotion to animals was that he found the bloody work in his father's tannery was almost unbearable. Jesse understood and did not insist, but of course that did not excuse Hiram from other chores. "I did not like to work," Grant says in the *Memoirs*, "but I did as much of it, while young, as grown men can be hired to do these days, and attended school at the same time."

For the rest, Hiram was a somewhat unprepossessing boy, short, careless of dress, tone-deaf, and schooled in only the basic social graces. He had no very high opinion of himself and took it for granted that he was never meant to go to college.

But Jesse made no such assumption. Unknown to his son, he pulled some political strings and got the local Congressman to apply — successfully — for Hiram's admission to West Point. Hiram was appalled, insisted that he was not up to the Military Academy's academic standards, and at first refused to go. But his qualms were no proof against Jesse's iron will and the offer of a free education, and in May 1839 Hiram duly set out on the long trip to New York. He had never before ventured so far from home and, indeed, had never before been on a railroad train. (Hurtling along at 12 miles-per-hour, he "thought the perfection of rapid transit had been reached.")

He arrived at West Point at the end of the month and two weeks later ("very much to my surprise") passed the entrance exam easily. But he was still not reconciled to his fate. As he

notes in the *Memoirs*: "A military life had no charms for me, and I had not the faintest idea of staying in the army even if I should be graduated, which I did not expect." Others shared his misgivings. One upperclassman later wrote of him, "A more unpromising boy never entered the Academy": the writer was William Tecumseh Sherman.

Due to a clerical error, Hiram was enrolled in West Point as "Ulysses Simpson Grant," and when he protested he was told he had better accept his new name because too much paperwork would be needed to correct the mistake. His amused classmates speculated that his new initials, U.S., must stand for "Uncle Sam," and promptly began calling him "Sam," a nickname by which he would be known in army circles for a good many years thereafter.

Grant's academic career at West Point was respectable, though hardly distinguished. If he can be said to have had an aptitude, it was for mathematics, but he was an idle student and never really excelled in anything, save possibly in the number of demerits he collected for untidiness and inattention. Yet those (relatively few) classmates who knew him intimately had considerable respect for his intelligence: they thought he did amazingly well in his recitations and examinations, considering how little he studied for them. He was graduated 21st in a class of 39.

He had hoped for a posting to the cavalry, but there were few available openings, and neither his West Point grades nor his social connections were such as to recommend him for one of these plums. So, instead, he was assigned to the 4th Infantry

Regiment as a brevet 2nd lieutenant, and in September 1843 he reported to Jefferson Barracks in St. Louis to begin what he still assumed would be his brief career in the U.S. Army.

The Jefferson Barracks proved to be a surprisingly pleasant introduction to army life. It was a well-run, unexceptionally military post, yet it left its officers plenty of free time to enjoy themselves. Increasingly, Grant found himself spending his off-hours at 5-mile-distant White Haven, the plantation-like home of one of his West Point roommates, Frederick Dent. From the first, Grant got on well with all the Dent family and, in time, better than well with Frederick's oldest sister, Julia, then 17. By 1844 Grant's and Julia's relationship had matured to a point where it probably would have been only a matter of time before Grant proposed, but, as luck would have it, international events contrived both to hasten their engagement and postpone their marriage.

For nearly a decade U.S.-Mexican relations had been strained by the issue of Texas. In 1836 the "Anglo"-dominated Mexican province of Texas had declared its independence and had successfully resisted all Mexican attempts to reintegrate it by force. Soon the Texans were petitioning Washington for admission into the United States, but the Van Buren and (for a time) Tyler administrations had resisted the idea, partly for fear of provoking Mexico, which did not recognize Texan sovereignty, and partly because the admission of the new state could seriously complicate the precarious Congressional balance between pro- and anti-slavery states, by then the most envenomed issue in American national politics. But by 1844 a

OPPOSITE LEFT: Future CSA General Cadmus Wilcox was a member of Grant's wedding in 1848. He would fight Grant during the 1864-65 campaign and would surrender with Lee at Appomattox Court House.

OPPOSITE RIGHT: President James K. Polk in 1845.

BELOW: Grant with Julia and their four children *c.* 1865. Grant was a devoted family man, and it was for the sake of his family's financial security that, near the end of his life, he reluctantly agreed to write his personal memoirs for publication by his friend Mark Twain.

passion for territorial aggrandizement was fulminating in the U.S., and popular sentiment in favor of the annexation of Texas had grown so strong that it was now less a question of ''if'' than of ''when''. To many Americans, the prospect of war with Mexico now seemed less a deterrent than an opportunity.

Texas was formally annexed at the beginning of James K. Polk's administration in 1845, and in March Grant's regiment was ordered to the western (*ie.*, Texan) border of Louisiana. Before leaving, Grant hurriedly formalized his engagement to Julia, who promised to marry him on his return. (She would have to wait more than three years, which she did, unwaveringly.) Grant was also obliged to shelve plans he had been working on

to secure a West Point teaching assignment, something he saw as a first step in a process of gradually breaking his ties with the army. As for his opinion of the cause of these disruptions, Grant says bluntly in his *Memoirs*: "For myself, I was bitterly opposed to [the annexation], and to this day regard the war, which resulted, as one of the most unjust ever waged by a stronger against a weaker nation."

The Mexicans, though very angry, did not make the annexation a *casus belli*, nor did they do so when General Zachary Taylor's U.S. "Army of Occupation" (of which the 4th Infantry was a part) arrived in Texas in early 1846. But matters changed drastically when Taylor then led his troops south of the Neuces River, which the Mexicans regarded as the southern border of Texas, and occupied the large strip of land that lay between it and the Rio Grande. Washington offered the barely plausible explanation that most Texans considered the Rio Grande to be their "natural" border, but few people took this seriously, least of all Grant. "We were sent to provoke a fight," he wrote, "but it was essential that Mexico should commence it."

Faced with what amounted to a de facto invasion, the Mexicans of course commenced it, beginning by shelling a fort the Americans had hastily built upon arriving at the left bank of the Rio Grande. In early May they directly challenged Taylor's army at the Battle of Palo Alto, which the better-equipped Americans easily won.

Palo Alto was Grant's first real taste of combat. In the *Memoirs* he tends to make light of it. (Speaking of the smooth-bore flintlock muskets used by both sides, he remarks, "At the distance of a few hundred yards a man might fire at you all day

ABOVE: General Zachary Taylor, under whom Grant first served in Mexico.

BELOW: Taylor takes Monterrey on September 24, 1846.

OPPOSITE: Fought immediately after the opening battle of Palo Alto, Resaca de la Palma was Grant's second taste of battle in the Mexican War.

without your finding it out.'') But Palo Alto was a bloody enough encounter, and it would be followed by many worse, for it was taken in Washington as the signal that the full-fledged invasion of Mexico could now begin.

Taylor pursued the retreating Mexican army for 200 miles southwest toward Monterrey, which he took, after hard fighting, on September 24. Soon thereafter the 4th Infantry, along with many other units, was detached from Taylor's command and ordered to return to the mouth of the Rio Grande, where General Winfield Scott was assembling another invasion force that was to be transported by sea far to the south to the coastal city of Vera Cruz, gateway to Mexico City itself. Grant had mixed feelings about leaving Taylor's army. He understood the importance of Scott's operation, but he had come to admire Taylor's competence and unpretentious, ''rough and ready'' style of command. And in some degree Taylor seems to have reciprocated the feeling: once, while watching Grant working with his men waist-deep in water to clear some obstruction, Taylor remarked, ''I wish I had more officers like Grant, . . . ready to set a personal example when needed.'' In any case, Grant's own style of command would one day much resemble Taylor's.

Scott's amphibious force arrived at Vera Cruz in mid-March 1847 and took the city after a two-week siege. Then, against large defending forces commanded by General Antonio López de Santa Anna, Scott began to fight his way inland towards the Mexican capital. There were sharp clashes all along the way, beginning at Cerro Gordo on April 18, and Scott did not reach the vicinity of Mexico City until August. He then had to fight a series of fierce battles in the city's suburbs – at El Pedregal, Contraras, Cherubusco, Molino, del Rey, Chapultepec, San Cosme, and elsewhere – and did not finally force Santa Anna to surrender Mexico City until September 17. By the Treaty of Guadalupe Hidalgo, signed the following February, the United States acquired from Mexico not only the Rio Grande boundary but present-day New Mexico, Arizona, and California as well. It had been a brilliantly successful, if shameful, war.

Grant had distinguished himself repeatedly during all this hard fighting (for example, his idea of setting up a mountain howitzer in a church belfry at San Cosme had contributed much to the winning of the battle) and had risen to the rank of 1st lieutenant by the time the war ended. He had also gotten to know a great many of the U.S. Army officers of his generation, something that would prove invaluable to him in his next war.

He served several more months in Mexico, finally returning to the United States in mid-1848 and marrying Julia on August 22. Despite some misgivings, he decided to stay on for a while in the peacetime army, and he and Julia spent the next three-and-a-half (low-paid but otherwise happy) years at posts in New York and Michigan. In 1852 he was ordered to San Francisco, and, since the trip was arduous and Julia was expecting their second child, it was agreed that he would go on ahead, she to join him at some future date when he had found adequate living quarters for his burgeoning family.

When Grant arrived in California in September 1852 he found it still in the last throes of the Great Gold Rush. Prices were (certainly by the standards of army pay) astronomical, and Grant

LEFT: In the fighting in the outskirts of Mexico City in 1847, Grant clears neighboring rooftops of enemy snipers by mounting a howitzer in the belfry of a church.

OPPOSITE: Perhaps the most colorful of the volunteer units mobilized by both sides at the start of the Civil War were the fancifully dressed Zouaves. Here, a corps of the Pennsylvania Zouaves parades in Philadelphia in 1861.

sadly concluded that it would be a long while before he could afford to bring his family west. To complicate matters, he was soon moved out of San Francisco to a succession of remote wilderness posts, first to Fort Vancouver on the Columbia River and then, in 1853, to Humbolt Bay, 250 miles north of San Francisco. Lonely, bored, and disconsolate, he began to drink more than he should, and this brought to a head a conflict that had been simmering between him and his superior at Humbolt Bay. In a stormy interview this officer told Grant that he would court martial him unless he resigned his commission. It was almost certainly an idle threat, but Grant treated it as though it were serious and promptly resigned from the army.

He was, in fact, delighted to return to Julia and his two sons, but he now also had to face the problem of how to make a living in a civilian world he had not known since he entered West Point 14 years earlier. At first he tried farming some land that had been left to Julia outside St. Louis, but luck was against him. Even if he had been an experienced farmer (which he certainly was not), his lack of capitalization would probably have made it impossible for him to ride out the wave of misfortunes that beset him: a succession of poor growing-years, a financial panic, and, finally, a debilitating illness. Defeated at last, he sold off his crops, stock, and farming utensils in 1858 and next tried his hand in a real estate partnership in St. Louis. But he was an even poorer businessman than he was a farmer, and the venture collapsed within a year. By 1860 he had been reduced to accepting a minor clerkship in a leather goods store owned by his father in Galena, Illinois.

This pattern of honorable failure in civilian life would, in effect, be repeated years later during Grant's two terms as President of the United States (1869-1877). In the realms of politics, business, and even personal relations he would be a perennial naïf, never quite grasping the inner rules of the games being played and guilelessly trusting in people whose primary motive was to exploit him. Yet in the military world – the world of which he had always been so suspicious and had left so easily – he had displayed none of these defects. Only in that world, it seems, could his true talents (and that is too mild a word for them) flourish. In 1860, to be sure, he was almost certainly unaware that he had any such talents. But he, and the world, were about to find out otherwise.

In 1860 the witch's brew of moral, economic, and political conflicts to which the institution of slavery had given rise finally boiled over. The precipitating event was the election in November of Abraham Lincoln, the presidential candidate of the anti-slavery Republican Party. Lincoln's election appalled the South and convinced many Southerners that they could no longer live within the constitutional framework of the United States. A month later South Carolina seceded from the Union, and by early 1861 six other Southern states had followed suit and had joined South Carolina in forming a rival American government, the Confederate States of America. In April, Confederate troops bombarded and captured Federal Fort Sumter in Charleston harbor, an act that plunged the American commonwealth into civil war.

Grant was electrified by these events, hastened to help recruit troops for the Union cause, and applied to the Secretary of War for reinstatement in the U.S. Army. Washington, at first having little interest in ex-Captain Grant, was slow to respond, but the Governor of Illinois in the meantime awarded Grant a militia colonelcy and the command of a regiment of raw volunteers, the 21st Illinois, which he duly set about training.

As the size of the Union army grew, Washington became aware that it was facing a severe shortage of trained officers, many West Pointers having gravitated to the Confederate side. In July 1861 the President submitted to Congress names of 26 men to be created U.S. Army brigadier generals. An Illinois Congressman named Washburn saw to it that Grant's name was on the list, and, to Grant's amazed gratification, Congress confirmed his appointment. Had he remained in the regular army instead of resigning, such a leap in promotion would have been virtually unthinkable.

Grant did not, however, rate high enough in Washington's estimation to be assigned to what was then regarded as the most important theater of war, the hotly contested stretch of countryside that lay between Washington and the Confederate capital of Richmond, Virginia. This was probably just as well, for not only would the Union suffer an almost unbroken series of

military defeats in the East for the remainder of 1861 and all through 1862, the true strategic pivot of the war lay just where Grant was, in the West. And although virtually no one grasped this truth in 1861, Grant did.

Grant's first major assignment was to command the military headquarters at Cairo, in southern Illinois, where the Ohio River joins the Mississippi. Across the Ohio from Cairo lies the western tip of Kentucky, one of the few Southern states that had elected to remain within the Union and into which Confederate forces from Tennessee were already beginning to pour. Grant at once saw the danger — both political and strategic — and he quickly moved to occupy Padukah, Kentucky, located at the junction of the Ohio and Tennessee rivers, in order to block any Confederate invasion route north via the Tennessee. Next, in November, seizing on an order to make a "demonstration" against the Mississippi River town of Belmont, Missouri, Grant attacked the place, with the intention of then going on to occupy Columbus, Kentucky, across the river, before Confederate forces under General Leonidas Polk could so so. In the event, the fighting at Belmont was sharper than anticipated, and Grant's designs on Columbus were frustrated. Even so, Polk felt sufficiently threatened so that when he did occupy Columbus he felt himself pinned there and unable to detach any troops to assist Confederate operations elsewhere.

Shortly after the Battle of Belmont, Washington divided overall command in the West between General Henry W. Halleck, who was given the Department of the Missouri (from Arkansas to western Kentucky and points north), and General Don Carlos Buell, who was given the Department of the Ohio (Kentucky east of the Cumberland and Tennessee rivers). Halleck, who was Grant's immediate superior, was about as difficult a man to work for as anyone could wish, but at least he was a fairly good theoretical strategist, and Grant approved of his preference for trying to conduct initial offensive operations southward along

the Tennessee–Cumberland route, rather than along the Mississippi. This route was, however, blocked almost at its beginning by three strong Confederate river forts — Heiman, Henry, and Donelson — and when Grant suggested to Halleck that he thought he could capture the forts, Halleck treated the proposal as preposterous. Only when Flag Officer Andrew Hull Foote, commander of the U.S. Navy's riverine gunboat squadron in the area, announced his support of Grant's project did Halleck grudgingly relent. The operation — the first of an increasingly brilliant string of Grant victories — was planned to begin early in February 1862. In the chapter that follows Grant describes what happened.

OPPOSITE TOP: The event that finally drove the Southern states to secession was the 1860 election of Republican candidate Abraham Lincoln.

OPPOSITE: Secession becomes war: South Carolina attacks Fort Sumter in April 1861.

TOP RIGHT: Confederate Bishop-cum-General Leonidas Polk.

RIGHT: Union General Don Carlos Buell's Army of the Ohio in 1862.

Chapter I

Fort Henry and Fort Donelson

Fort Henry occupies a bend in the river which gave the guns in the water battery a direct fire down the stream. The camp outside the fort was intrenched, with rifle pits and outworks two miles back on the road to Donelson and Dover. The garrison of the fort and camp was about 2,800, with strong reinforcements from Donelson halted some miles out. There were seventeen heavy guns in the fort. The river was very high, the banks being overflowed except where the bluffs come to the water's edge. A portion of the ground on which Fort Henry stood was two feet deep in water. Below, the water extended into the woods several hundred yards back from the bank on the east side. On the west bank Fort Heiman stood on high ground, completely

commanding Fort Henry. The distance from Fort Henry to Donelson is but eleven miles. The two positions were so important to the enemy, *as he saw his interest*, that it was natural to suppose that reinforcements would come from every quarter from which they could be got. Prompt action on our part was imperative.

The plan was for the troops and gunboats to start at the same moment. The troops were to invest the garrison and the gunboats to attack the fort at close quarters. General [Charles F.] Smith was to land a brigade of his division on the west bank during the night of the 5th and get it in rear of Heiman.

At the hour designated the troops and gunboats started. General Smith found Fort Heiman had been evacuated before his men

Grant as a Lieutenant general in 1864. His elevation to the highest military rank his country could confer was all but unimaginable two years earlier. It was the capture of forts Henry and Donelson that began his meteoric rise.

18

arrived. The gunboats soon engaged the water batteries at very close quarters, but the troops which were to invest Fort Henry were delayed for want of roads, as well as by the dense forest and the high water in what would in dry weather have been unimportant beds of streams. This delay made no difference in the result. On our first appearance [Confederate General Lloyd] Tilghman had sent his entire command, with the exception of about one hundred men left to man the guns in the fort, to the outworks on the road to Dover and Donelson, so as to have them out of range of the guns of our navy; and before any attack on the 6th he had ordered them to retreat on Donelson. He stated in his subsequent report that the defence was intended solely to give his troops time to make their escape.

Tilghman was captured with his staff and ninety men, as well as the armament of the fort, the ammunition and whatever stores were there. Our cavalry pursued the retreating column towards Donelson and picked up two guns and a few stragglers; but the enemy had so much the start, that the pursuing force did not get in sight of any except the stragglers.

All the gunboats engaged were hit many times. The damage, however, beyond what could be repaired by a small expenditure of money, was slight, except to the *Essex*. A shell penetrated the boiler of that vessel and exploded it, killing and wounding forty-eight men, nineteen of whom were soldiers who had been detailed to act with the navy. On several occasions during the war such details were made when the complement of men with the navy was insufficient for the duty before them. After the fall of Fort Henry Captain [S.L.] Phelps, commanding the iron-clad *Carondelet*, at my request ascended the Tennessee River and thoroughly destroyed the bridge of the Memphis and Ohio Railroad. . . .

On the 7th, the day after the fall of Fort Henry, I took my staff and the cavalry – a part of one regiment – and made a reconnoissance to within about a mile of the outer line of works at Donelson. I had known General [Gideon] Pillow in Mexico, and judged that with any force, no matter how small, I could march up to within gunshot of any intrenchments he was given to hold. I said this to the officers of my staff at the time. I knew that [John B.] Floyd was in command, but he was no soldier, and I judged that he would yield to Pillow's pretensions. I met, as I ex-

LEFT: Charles Ferguson Smith was probably Grant's ablest lieutenant in the assault on forts Henry and Donelson. He would die soon thereafter of an injury received at Shiloh.

BELOW: Confederate General Gideon Pillow was second in command at Fort Donelson. He amply confirmed Grant's low opinion of his abilities when Grant attacked the fort.

pected, no opposition in making the reconnoissance and, besides learning the topography of the country on the way and around Fort Donelson, found that there were two roads available for marching; one leading to the village of Dover, the other to Donelson.

Fort Donelson is two miles north, or down the river, from Dover. The fort, as it stood in 1861, embraced about one hundred acres of land. On the east it fronted the Cumberland; to the north it faced Hickman's creek, a small stream which at the time was deep and wide because of the back-water from the river; on the south was another small

stream, or rather a ravine, opening into the Cumberland. This also was filled with backwater from the river. The fort stood on high ground, some of it as much as a hundred feet above the Cumberland. Strong protection to the heavy guns in the water batteries had been obtained by cutting away places for them in the bluff. To the west there was a line of rifle-pits some two miles back from the river at the farthest point. This line ran generally along the crest of high ground, but in one place crossed a ravine which opens into the river between the village and the fort. The ground inside and outside of this in-

LEFT: The U.S.S. *St. Louis* was the first of a series of ironclad river gunboats built for the Union navy by the engineer James Buchanan Eads. She was part of the squadron led by Andrew Hull Foote against Fort Donelson while Grant was attacking the place on land. Grant's respect for the Navy and readiness to work with it in combined operations was highly unusual among U.S. Army officers, and it would stand Grant in good stead in the Vicksburg Campaign.

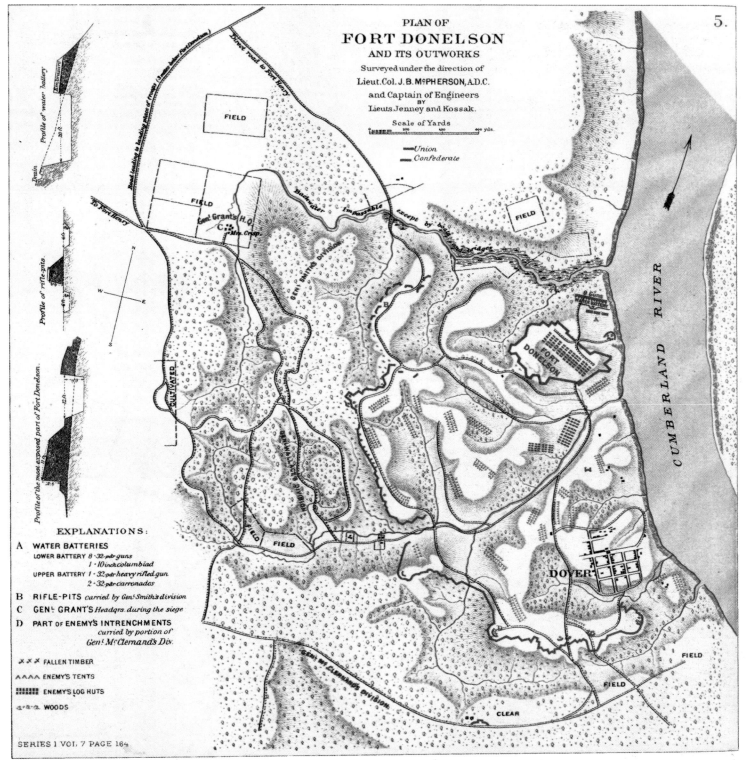

PLAN OF
FORT DONELSON
AND ITS OUTWORKS

Surveyed under the direction of
Lieut. Col. J. B. McPHERSON, A.D.C.
and Captain of Engineers
BY
Lieuts. Jenney and Kossak.

Scale of Yards

━━━ Union
━━━ Confederate

EXPLANATIONS:

A WATER BATTERIES
   LOWER BATTERY 8 · 32-pdr guns
             1 · 10 inch columbiad
   UPPER BATTERY 1 · 32-pdr heavy rifled gun
             2 · 32-pdr carronades

B RIFLE-PITS carried by Gen! Smith's division

C GEN! GRANT'S Headqrs. during the siege

D PART OF ENEMY'S INTRENCHMENTS
             carried by portion of
             Gen! McClernand's Div.

✗ ✗ ✗ FALLEN TIMBER

∧∧∧∧ ENEMY'S TENTS

▦▦▦▦ ENEMY'S LOG HUTS

⌾⌾⌾ WOODS

SERIES 1 VOL. 7 PAGE 164

trenched line was very broken and generally wooded. The trees outside of the rifle-pits had been cut down for a considerable way out, and had been felled so that their tops lay outwards from the intrenchments. The limbs had been trimmed and pointed, and thus formed an abatis in front of the greater part of the line. Outside of this intrenched line, and extending about half the entire length of it, is a ravine running north and south and opening into Hickman creek at a point north of the fort. The entire side of this ravine next to the works was one long abatis. . . .

I was very impatient to get to Fort Donelson because I knew the importance of the place to the enemy and supposed he would reinforce it rapidly. I felt that 15,000 men on the 8th would be more effective than 50,000 a month later. I asked Flag-officer [Andrew] Foote, therefore, to order his gunboats still about Cairo to proceed up the Cumberland River and not to wait for those gone to Eastport and Florence; but the others got back in time and we started on the 12th. I had moved [General John A.] McClernand out a few miles the night before so as to leave the road as free as possible. . . .

ABOVE: A contemporary U.S. Army map shows the position of opposing forces during the investment of Fort Donelson.

OPPOSITE: John B. Floyd, the confederate commander of Fort Donelson. Grant's contempt for Pillow, Floyd's second in command, was mild compared to his feelings about Floyd.

along the crest of the ridges. The artillery was protected by being sunk in the ground. The men who were not serving the guns were perfectly covered from fire on taking position a little back from the crest. The greatest suffering was from want of shelter. It was midwinter and during the siege we had rain and snow, thawing and freezing alternately. It would not do to allow camp-fires except far down the hill out of sight of the enemy, and it would not do to allow many of the troops to remain there at the same time. In the march over from Fort Henry numbers of the men had thrown away their blankets and overcoats. There was . . . much discomfort and . . . suffering.

During the 12th and 13th, and until the arrival of [General Lewis] Wallace and [Colonel] Thayer on the 14th, the National forces, composed of but 15,000 men, without intrenchments, confronted an intrenched army of 21,000, without conflict further than what was brought on by ourselves. Only one gunboat had arrived. There was a little skirmishing each day, brought on by the movement of our troops in securing commanding positions; but there was no actual fighting during this time except once, on the 13th, in front of McClernand's command. That general had undertaken to capture a battery of the enemy which was annoying his men. Without orders or

ABOVE: Flag Officer Andrew Hull Foote, commander of the Navy's riverine flotilla and a staunch admirer and ally of General Grant.

RIGHT: General Lewis (Lew) Wallace, one of Grant's abler lieutenants at Donelson, later became famous as the author of the novel *Ben Hur*.

I started from Fort Henry with 15,000 men, including eight batteries and part of a regiment of cavalry, and, meeting with no obstruction to detain us, the advance arrived in front of the enemy by noon. That afternoon and the next day were spent in taking up ground to make the investment as complete as possible. . . . The troops were not intrenched, but the nature of the ground was such that they were just as well protected from the fire of the enemy as if rifle-pits had been thrown up. Our line was generally

authority he sent three regiments to make the assault. The battery was in the main line of the enemy, which was defended by his whole army present. Of course the assault was a failure, and of course the loss on our side was great for the number of men engaged. . . .

During the night of the 13th Flag-officer Foote arrived with the iron-clads *St. Louis*, *Louisville* and *Pittsburg* and the wooden gunboats *Tyler* and *Conestoga*, convoying Thayer's brigade. On the morning of the 14th Thayer was landed. Wallace, whom I had ordered over from Fort Henry, also arrived about the same time. . . .

The plan was for the troops to hold the enemy within his lines, while the gunboats should attack the water batteries at close quarters and silence his guns if possible. Some of the gunboats were to run the batteries, get above the fort and above the village of Dover. . . .

By three in the afternoon of the 14th Flag-officer Foote was ready, and advanced upon the water batteries with his entire fleet. After coming in range of the batteries of the enemy the advance was slow, but a constant fire was delivered from every gun that could be brought to bear upon the fort. I occupied a position on shore from which I could see the advancing navy. The leading boat got within a very short distance of the water battery, not further off I think than two hundred yards, and I soon saw one and then another of them dropping down the river, visibly disabled. Then the whole fleet followed and the engagement closed for the day. The gunboat which Flag-officer Foote was on, besides having been hit about sixty times, several of the shots passing through near the waterline, had a shot enter the pilot-house which killed the pilot, carried away the wheel and wounded the flag-officer himself. The tiller-

ropes of another vessel were carried away and she, too, dropped helplessly back. Two others had their pilot-houses so injured that they scarcely formed a protection to the men at the wheel.

The enemy had evidently been much demoralized by the assault, but they were jubilant when they saw the disabled vessels

TOP: The naval attack on Fort Donelson, led by *St. Louis*.

ABOVE: Mortimer Leggett, who led a regiment of green Ohio volunteers against Donelson, later became a distinguished Union General.

dropping down the river entirely out of control of the men on board. Of course I only witnessed the falling back of our gunboats and felt sad enough at the time over the repulse. Subsequent reports, now published, show that the enemy telegraphed a great victory to Richmond. The sun went down on the night of the 14th of February, 1862, leaving the army confronting Fort Donelson anything but comforted over the prospects. The weather had turned intensely cold; the men were without tents and could not keep up fires where most of them had to stay, and, as previously stated, many had thrown away their overcoats and blankets. Two of the strongest of our gunboats had been disabled, presumably beyond the possibility of rendering any present assistance. I retired this night not knowing but that I would have to intrench my position, and bring up tents for the men or build huts under the cover of the hills.

On the morning of the 15th, before it was yet broad day, a messenger from Flag-officer Foote handed me a note, expressing a desire to see me on the flag-ship and saying that he had been injured the day before so much that he could not come himself to me. I at once made my preparations for starting. . . .

When I reached the fleet I found the flag-ship was anchored out in the stream. A small boat, however, awaited my arrival and I was soon on board with the flag-officer. He explained to me in short the condition in which he was left by the engagement of the evening before, and suggested that I should intrench while he returned to Mound City with his disabled boats, expressing at the time the belief that he could have the necessary repairs made and be back in ten days. I saw the absolute necessity of his gunboats going into hospital and did not know but I should be forced to the alternative of going

through a siege. But the enemy relieved me from this necessity. . . .

Just as I landed I met Captain Hillyer of my staff, white with fear, not for his personal safety, but for the safety of the National troops. He said the enemy had come out of his lines in full force and attacked and scattered McClernand's division, which was in full retreat. The roads, as I have said, were unfit for making fast time, but I got to my command as soon as possible. . . .

I saw everything favorable for us along the line of our left and centre. When I came to the right appearances were different. The enemy had come out in full force to cut his way out and make his escape. McClernand's division had to bear the brunt of the attack from this combined force. His men had stood up gallantly until the ammunition in their cartridge-boxes gave out. There was abundance of ammunition near by lying on the ground in boxes, but at that stage of the war it was not all of our commanders of regiments, brigades, or even divisions, who had been educated up to the point of seeing that their men were constantly supplied with ammunition during an engagement. When the men found themselves without ammunition they could not stand up against troops who seemed to have plenty of it. The division broke and a portion fled, but most of the men, as they were pursued, only fell back out of range of the fire of the enemy. It must have been about this time that Thayer pushed his brigade in between the enemy and those of our troops that were without ammunition. At all events the enemy fell back within his intrenchments and was there when I got on the field.

I saw the men standing in knots talking in the most excited manner. No officer seemed to be giving any directions. The soldiers had their muskets, but no ammunition, while

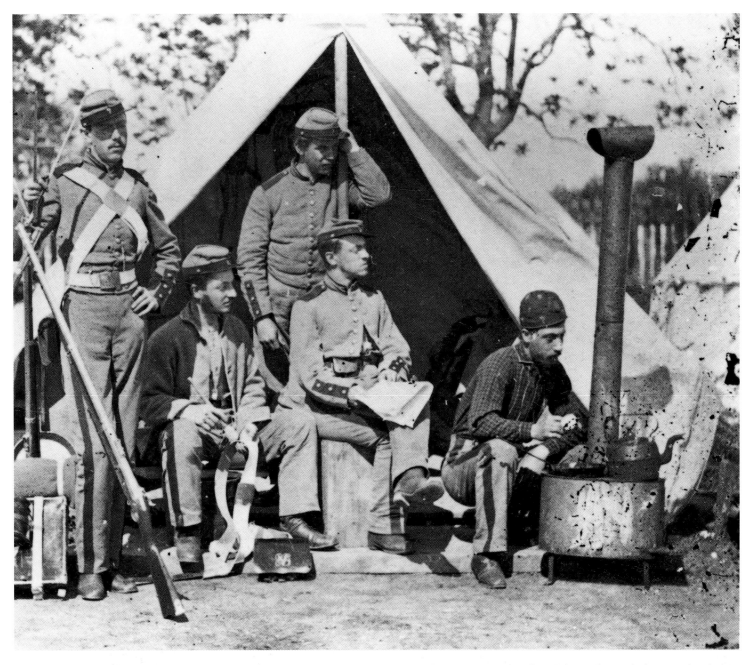

there were tons of it close at hand. I heard some of the men say that the enemy had come out with knapsacks, and haversacks filled with rations. They seemed to think this indicated a determination on his part to stay out and fight just as long as the provisions held out. I turned to Colonel J. D. Webster, of my staff, who was with me, and said: "Some of our men are pretty badly demoralized, but the enemy must be more so, for he has attempted to force his way out, but has fallen back: the one who attacks first now will be victorious and the enemy will have to be in a hurry if he gets ahead of me." . . . I directed Colonel Webster to ride with me and call out to the men as we passed: "Fill your cartridge-boxes, quick, and get into line; the enemy is trying to escape and he must not be permitted to do so." This acted like a charm. The men only wanted some one to give them a command. We rode rapidly to Smith's quarters, when I explained the situation to him and directed him to charge the enemy's works in his front with his whole division, saying at the same time that he would find nothing but a very thin line to contend with. The general was off in an incredibly short time, going in advance himself to keep his men from firing while they were working their way through the abatis intervening between them and the enemy. The outer line of rifle-pits was passed, and the night of the 15th General Smith, with much of his division, bivouacked within the lines of the enemy. There was now no doubt but that the Confederates must surrender or be captured the next day.

There seems from subsequent accounts to have been much consternation, particularly among the officers of high rank, in

ABOVE: A vignette of typical Union army camp life in 1862. The men shown here belong to the 7th New York militia.

OPPOSITE: Grant's campaign against the Cumberland River forts established his name as a "fighting general." This modern portrait by N. C. Wyeth well conveys that facet of Grant's complex personality.

29

Dover during the night of the 15th. General Floyd, the commanding officer, who was a man of talent enough for any civil position, was no soldier and, possibly, did not possess the elements of one. He was further unfitted for command, for the reason that his conscience must have troubled him and made him afraid. As Secretary of War he had taken a solemn oath to maintain the Constitution of the United States and to uphold the same against all its enemies. He had betrayed that trust. As Secretary of War he was reported through the northern press to have scattered the little army the country had so that the most of it could be picked up in detail when secession occurred. About a year before leaving the Cabinet he had removed arms from northern to southern arsenals. He continued in the Cabinet of President Buchanan until about the 1st of January, 1861, while he was working vigilantly for the establishment of a confederacy made out of United States territory. Well may he have been afraid to fall into the hands of National troops. He would no doubt have been tried for misappropriating public property, if not for treason, had he been captured. General Pillow, next in command, was conceited, and prided himself much on his services in the Mexican war. He telegraphed to General [Albert S.] Johnston, at Nashville, after our men were within the rebel rifle-pits, and almost on the eve of his making his escape, that the Southern troops had had great success all day. Johnston forwarded the dispatch to Richmond. While the authorities at the capital were reading it Floyd and Pillow were fugitives.

A council of war was held by the enemy at which all agreed that it would be impossible

OPPOSITE: This view of the 94th Pennsylvania at drill gives a good idea of the size of a typical regiment of the Union army's infantry.

BELOW: The final assault on Fort Donelson as imagined by the printmakers Kurz & Allison.

to hold out longer. General [Simon Bolivar] Buckner, who was third in rank in the garrison but much the most capable soldier, seems to have regarded it a duty to hold the fort until the general commanding the department, A. S. Johnston, should get back to his headquarters at Nashville. Buckner's report shows, however, that he considered Donelson lost and that any attempt to hold the place longer would be at the sacrifice of the command. Being assured that Johnston was already in Nashville, Buckner too agreed that surrender was the proper thing. Floyd turned over the command to Pillow, who declined it. It then devolved upon Buckner, who accepted the responsibility of the position. Floyd and Pillow took possession of all the river transports at Dover and before morning both were on their way to Nashville, with the brigade formerly commanded by Floyd and some other troops, in all about 3,000. Some marched up the east bank of the Cumberland; others went on the steamers. During the night (N.B.) Forrest also, with his cavalry and some other troops, about a thousand in all, made their way out, passing between our right and the river. They had to ford or swim over the backwater in the little creek just south of Dover.

Before daylight General Smith brought to me the following letter from General Buckner:

> SIR:- In consideration of all the circumstances governing the present situation of affairs at this station, I propose to the Commanding Officer of the Federal forces the appointment of Commissioners to agree upon terms of capitulation of the forces and fort under my command, and in that view suggest an armistice until 12 o'clock to-day.
>
> I am, sir, very respectfully,
> Your ob't se'v't,
> S. B. BUCKNER

To this I responded as follows:

> SIR:- Yours of this date, proposing armistice and appointment of Commissioners to settle terms of capitulation, is just received. No terms except an unconditional and immediate surrender can be accepted. I propose to move immediately upon your works.
>
> I am, sir, very respectfully,
> Your ob't se'v't,
> U. S. GRANT

To this I received the following reply:

> SIR:- The distribution of the forces under my command, incident to an unexpected change of commanders, and the overwhelming force under your command, compel me, notwithstanding the brilliant success of the Confederate arms yesterday, to accept the ungenerous and unchivalrous terms which you propose.
>
> I am, sir,
> Your ob't se'v't,
> S. B. BUCKNER

I had been at West Point three years with Buckner and afterwards served with him in the army, so that we were quite well acquainted. In the course of our conversation, which was very friendly, he said to me that if he had been in command I would not have got up to Donelson as easily as I did. I told him that if he had been in command I should not have tried in the way I did: I had invested their lines with a smaller force than they had to defend them, and at the same time had sent a brigade full 5,000 strong, around by water; I had relied very much upon their commander to allow me to come safely up to the outside of their works. . . .

BELOW: Confederate General Simon Bolivar Buckner succeeded to the command of Fort Donelson after his two superiors fled. An old friend of Grant, he expected that Grant would offer him lenient surrender terms. Instead, Grant's terms were flatly unconditional.

ABOVE: The railway station at Corinth, Mississippi. Because Grant's superiors failed to follow up his victory over the river forts, the enemy was able to regroup in Corinth and mount the counterstroke that resulted in the Battle of Shiloh in early April.

LEFT: Bushrod R. Johnson was among the senior Confederate officers who escaped from Fort Donelson. He would clash with Grant again less than two months later at Shiloh.

33

Chapter II

Shiloh

The news of the fall of forts Henry and Donelson was received with delight in the victory-starved North and served to focus national attention for the first time on "Unconditional Surrender" Grant, who was promptly promoted to the grade of major-general. Grant was convinced – then, and to the end of his days – that if the capture of the two strategically-located river forts had quickly been followed up with a series of coordinated Federal strikes at Chattanooga, Corinth, Memphis, and Vicksburg, virtually all of the Confederacy west of the Alleghenies might have fallen to the Union in 1862. But such daring thinking was beyond the grasp of the plodding, ungracious Halleck. Instead, Halleck took no coherent action, set up a great clamor for reinforcements, and even found occasion to pick a petty quarrel with Grant and to remove him – fortunately, only temporarily – from his command. In the meantime, the enemy was granted precious time to regroup his armies and to fortify new positions. By mid-March, when Grant was restored to his command of the District of Cairo, the Confederates had assembled a considerable army in Corinth, in northern Mississippi, under the command of the redoubtable Albert Sidney Johnston and his celebrated lieutenant P. G. T. Beauregard. It was against this force that Grant, whose troops were then centered on Savannah, in southern Tennessee, was now belatedly ordered to move. But Johnston moved even Faster: the result would be the bloodiest battle yet fought in the Western Hemisphere.

RIGHT: Don Carlos Buell, the commander of the Department of the Ohio, whose troops were to join with those of Grant for the assault on the enemy forces in Corinth.

OPPOSITE: Henry W. Halleck, overall, commander of Union armies in the West, was a constant thorn in Grant's side, failing to follow up on Grant's victories and forever picking quarrels with him.

When I reassumed command on the 17th of March I found the army divided, about half being on the east bank of the Tennessee at Savannah, while one division was at Crump's landing on the west bank about four miles higher up, and the remainder at Pittsburg landing, five miles above Crump's. The enemy was in force at Corinth, the junction of the two most important railroads in the Mississippi valley – one connecting Memphis and the Mississippi River with the East, and the other leading south to all the cotton states. Still another railroad connects Corinth with Jackson, in west Tennessee. If we obtained possession of Corinth the enemy would have no railroad for the transportation of armies or supplies until that running east from Vicksburg was reached. It was the great strategic position at the West between the Tennessee and the Mississippi rivers and between Nashville and Vicksburg.

I at once put all the troops at Savannah in motion for Pittsburg landing, knowing that the enemy was fortifying at Corinth and

collecting an army there under Johnston. It was my expectation to march against that army as soon as [General Don Carlos] Buell, who had been ordered to reinforce me with the Army of the Ohio, should arrive; and the west bank of the river was the place to start from. . . .

On the 17th of March the army on the Tennessee River consisted of five divisions, commanded respectively by Generals C. F. Smith, [J. A.] McClernand, L. Wallace, [S.] Hurlbut, and [W. T.] Sherman. General W. H. L. Wallace was temporarily in command of Smith's division, General Smith, as I have said, being confined to his bed. Reinforcements were arriving daily and as they came up they were organized, first into brigades, then into a division, and the command given to General [Benjamin] Prentiss, who had been ordered to report to me. General Buell was on his way from Nashville with 40,000 veterans. . . .

At this time I generally spent the day at Pittsburg and returned to Savannah in the evening. I was intending to remove my headquarters to Pittsburg, but Buell was expected daily and would come in at Savannah. I remained at this point, therefore, a few

days longer than I otherwise should have done, in order to meet him on his arrival. The skirmishing in our front, however, had been so continuous from about the 3d of April that I did not leave Pittsburg each night until an hour when I felt there would be no further danger before the morning. . . .

On the 5th General [William] Nelson, with a division of Buell's army, arrived at Savannah and I ordered him to move up the east bank of the river, to be in a position where he could be ferried over to Crump's landing or Pittsburg as occasion required. I had learned that General Buell himself would be at Savannah the next day, and desired to meet me on his arrival. . . . While I was at breakfast, however, heavy firing was heard in the direction of Pittsburg landing, and I hastened there, sending a hurried note to Buell informing him of the reason why I could not meet him at Savannah.

Up to that time I had felt by no means certain that Crump's landing might not be the point of attack. On reaching the front, however, about eight A.M., I found that the attack on Pittsburg was unmistakable. . . .

Some two of three miles from Pittsburg landing was a log meeting-house called

OPPOSITE: William Tecumseh Sherman. During the siege of Fort Donelson, Sherman, even though Grant's superior in rank, had offered to place himself under Grant's orders. At Shiloh he proved to be, by far, Grant's most effective lieutenant. From this early association was born what was to become one of the greatest partnerships in the history of warfare.

BELOW: Union troops foraging for food. The troops in this scene happened to belong to the division commanded by Benjamin Prentiss, soon to be the hero of the "Hornet's Nest" at Shiloh.

ABOVE: Grant's headquarters at Savannah, Tennessee, the center of his command before he began shifting his forces to Pittsburg Landing, where the Battle of Shiloh would erupt on April 6, 1862.

RIGHT: Union General William Nelson brought the first of Buell's troops (a division) that were to reinforce Grant at Pittsburg Landing.

OPPOSITE: The battlefield of Shiloh. This map is useful primarily as a geographic reference, since it depicts (somewhat self-servingly) only Buell's troop positions.

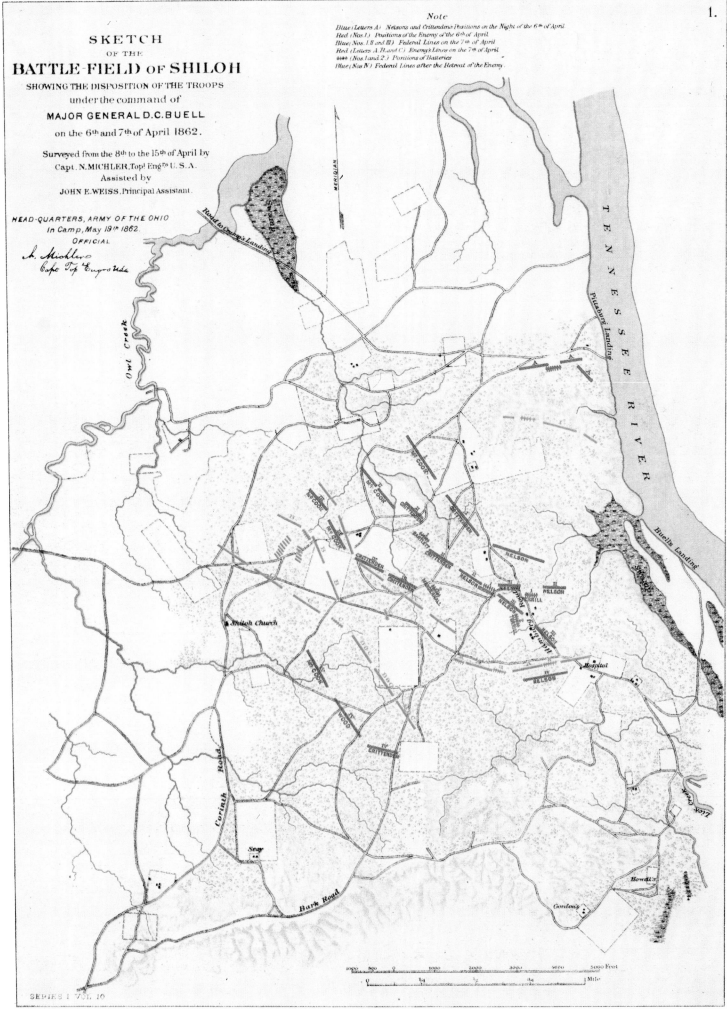

SKETCH
OF THE
BATTLE-FIELD OF SHILOH
SHOWING THE DISPOSITION OF THE TROOPS
under the command of
MAJOR GENERAL D.C. BUELL
on the 6th and 7th of April 1862.

Surveyed from the 8th to the 15th of April by
Capt. N. MICHLER, Topl Engrs U.S.A.
Assisted by
JOHN E. WEISS, Principal Assistant.

HEAD-QUARTERS, ARMY OF THE OHIO
In Camp, May 19th 1862.
OFFICIAL

Note
Blue (Letters A.) Nelsons and Crittendens Positions on the Night of the 6th of April.
Red (Nos. I.) Positions of the Enemy of the 6th of April.
Blue (Nos. I, II and III.) Federal Lines on the 7th of April.
Red (Letters A, B and C.) Enemy's Lines on the 7th of April.
(Nos. 1 and 2.) Positions of Batteries.
Blue (Nos. IV.) Federal Lines after the Retreat of the Enemy.

1.

SERIES I VOL 10

Shiloh. It stood on the ridge which divides the waters of Snake and Lick creeks, the former emptying into the Tennessee just north of Pittsburg landing, and the latter south. This point was the key to our position and was held by Sherman. His division was at that time wholly raw, no part of it ever having been in an engagement; but I thought this deficiency was more than made up by the superiority of the commander. McClernand was on Sherman's left, with troops that had been engaged at forts Henry and Donelson and were therefore veterans so far as western troops had become such at that stage of the war. Next to McClernand came Prentiss with a raw division, and on the extreme left, [Col. David] Stuart with one brigade of Sherman's division. Hurlbut was in rear of Prentiss, massed, and in reserve at the time of the onset. The division of General C. F. Smith was on the right, also in reserve. General Smith was still sick in bed at Savannah, but within hearing of our guns. His services would no doubt have been of inestimable value had his health permitted his presence. The command of his division devolved upon Brigadier-General W. H. L. Wallace, a most estimable and able officer;

a veteran too, for he had served a year in the Mexican war and had been with his command at Henry and Donelson. Wallace was mortally wounded in the the first day's engagement, and with the change of commanders . . . in the heat of battle the efficiency of his division was much weakened.

The position of our troops made a continuous line from Lick Creek on the left to Owl Creek, a branch of Snake Creek, on the right, facing nearly south and possibly a little west. The water in all these streams was very high at the time and contributed to protect our flanks. The enemy was compelled, therefore, to attack directly in front. This he did with great vigor, inflicting heavy losses on the National side, but suffering much heavier on his own.

The Confederate assaults were made with such a disregard of losses on their own side that our line of tents soon fell into their hands. The ground on which the battle was fought was undulating, heavily timbered with scattered clearings, the woods giving some protection to the troops on both sides. There was also considerable underbrush. A number of attempts were made by the enemy to turn our right flank, where Sher-

ABOVE: The Confederates begin their attack at Shiloh. In the party of officers on the right A. S. Johnston is shown in the center, with P.G.T. Beauregard on his right.

OPPOSITE: The home of Union General W.H.L. Wallace in Ottawa, Illinois, with his portrait and horse. Wallace, who had temporary command of the division of the ailing C.F. Smith, was killed on the first day of Shiloh.

RIGHT: "Bloody Shiloh." The scene here, of the second day of battle, shows a Wisconsin volunteer regiment charging a New Orleans battery.

man was posted, but every effort was repulsed with heavy loss. But the front attack was kept up so vigorously that, to prevent the success of these attempts to get on our flanks, the National troops were compelled, several times, to take position to the rear nearer Pittsburg landing. When the firing ceased at night the National line was all of a mile in rear of the position it had occupied in the morning.

In one of the backward moves, on the 6th, the division commanded by General Prentiss did not fall back with the others. This left his flanks exposed and enabled the enemy to capture him with about 2,200 of his officers and men. General [Adam] Badeau gives four o'clock of the 6th as about the time this capture took place. He may be right as to the time, but my recollection is that the hour was later. General Prentiss himself gave the hour as half-past five. I was with him, as I was with each of the division commanders that day, several times, and my recollection is that the last time I was with him was about half-past four, when his division was standing up firmly and the General was as cool as if expecting victory. But no matter whether it was four or later, the story that he and his command were surprised and captured in their camps is without any foundation whatever. If it had been true, as currently reported at the time and yet believed by thousands of people, that Prentiss and his division had been captured in their beds, there would not have been an all-day struggle, with the loss of thousands killed and wounded on the Confederate side.

BELOW: The "Hornet's Nest," a wooded area in the center of the Union line, became a focal point of resistance to the devastating Confederate surprise attack that struck Grant's army on the morning of April 6, the first day of the Battle of Shiloh.

With the single exception of a few minutes after the capture of Prentiss, a continuous and unbroken line was maintained all day from Snake Creek or its tributaries on the right to Lick Creek or the Tennessee on the left above Pittsburg. There was no hour during the day when there was not heavy firing and generally hard fighting at some

point on the line, but seldom at all points at the same time. . . .

During the whole of Sunday I was continuously engaged in passing from one part of the field to another, giving directions to division commanders. In thus moving along the line, however, I never deemed it important to stay long with Sherman. Although his troops were then under fire for the first time, their commander, by his constant presence with them, inspired a confidence in officers and men that enabled them to render services on that bloody battle-field worthy of the best of veterans. McClernand was next to Sherman, and the hardest fighting was in front of these two divisions. McClernand told me on that day, the 6th, that he profited much by having so able a commander supporting him. A casualty to Sherman that would have taken him from the field that day would have been a sad one for the troops engaged at Shiloh. And how near we came to this! On the 6th Sherman was shot twice, once in the hand, once in the shoulder, the ball cutting his coat and making a slight wound, and a third ball passed through his hat. In addition to this he had several horses shot during the day. . . .

The situation at the close of Sunday was as follows: along the top of the bluff just south of the log-house which stood at Pittsburg landing, Colonel J. D. Webster, of my staff, had arranged twenty of more pieces of artillery facing south or up the river. This line of artillery was on the crest of a hill overlooking a deep ravine opening into the Tennessee. Hurlbut with his division intact was on the right of this artillery, extending west and possibly a little north. McClernand came next in the general line, looking more to the west. His division was complete in its

RIGHT: Daniel Weisiger Adams was among the junior Southern officers who won distinction at Shiloh, where he led the 1st Louisiana Regulars. Adams would subsequently fight at Perryville, Murfreesboro, and Chickamauga.

BELOW: A noteworthy junior officer in the Union army at Shiloh was future President James Abram Garfield, then a brigadier general.

organization and ready for any duty. Sherman came next, his right extending to Snake Creek. His command, like the other two, was complete in its organization and ready, like its chief, for any service it might be called upon to render. All three divisions were, as a matter of course, more or less shattered and depleted in number from the terrible battle of the day. The division of W. H. L. Wallace, as much from the disorder arising from changes of division and brigade commanders, under heavy fire, as from any other cause, had lost its organization and did not occupy a place in the line as a division. Prentiss' command was gone as a division, many of its members having been killed, wounded or captured; but it had rendered valiant services before its final dispersal, and had contributed a good share to the defence of Shiloh. . . .

During the night of the 6th the remainder of Nelson's division, Buell's army, crossed the river and were ready to advance in the morning, forming the left wing. Two other divisions [J. L.] Crittenden's and [A. M.]

LEFT: Not yet a Confederate general officer at the time of the Battle of Shiloh was Basil Duke of the "Lexington Rifles". He would eventually become a brigadier general and a noted cavalry leader.

BELOW: This triple portrait is of Shiloh veteran James W. Denver, then a Union brigadier general. Denver, Colorado, is named for him

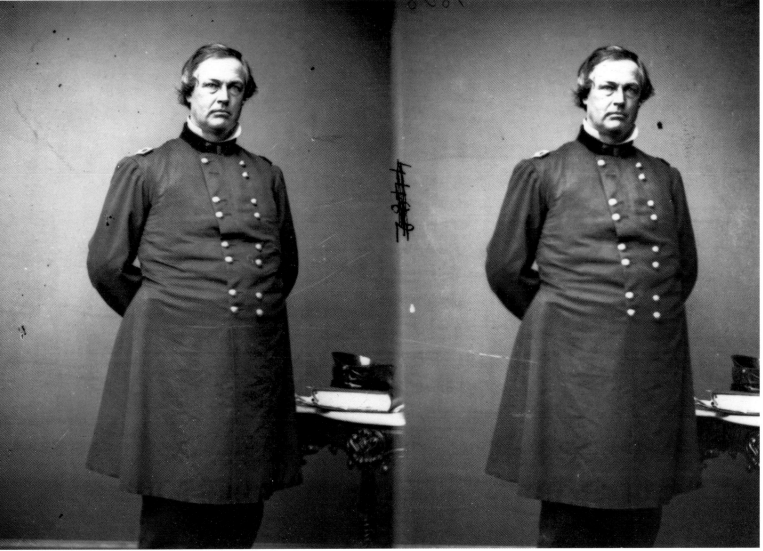

McCook's, came up the river from Savannah in the transports and were on the west bank early on the 7th. Buell commanded them in person. My command was thus nearly doubled in numbers and efficiency.

During the night rain fell in torrents and our troops were exposed to the storm without shelter. I made my headquarters under a tree a few hundred yards back from the river bank. My ankle was so much swollen from the fall of my horse the Friday night preceding, and the bruise was so painful, that I could get no rest. The drenching rain would have precluded the possibility of sleep without this additional cause. Some time after midnight, growing restive under the storm and the continuous pain, I moved back to the log-house under the bank. This had been taken as a hospital, and all night wounded men were being brought in, their wounds dressed, a leg or an arm amputated as the case might require, and everything being done to save life or alleviate suffering. The sight was more unendurable than encountering the enemy's fire, and I returned to my tree in the rain.

The advance on the morning of the 7th developed the enemy in the camps occupied by our troops before the battle began, more than a mile back from the most advanced position of the Confederates on the day before. It is known now that they had not yet learned of the arrival of Buell's command. Possibly they fell back so far to get the shel-

OPPOSITE: Union General T.J. Wood led one of the divisions in Buell's army that arrived too late to be of any real assistance to Grant at Shiloh. That Grant was unimpressed by Buell's performance is clear (though never explicit) from his comments in the *Memoirs*.

BELOW: Alexander McCook led one of the three divisions of Buell's reinforcing army that did arrive in time to play a useful role on the second day of the Battle of Shiloh.

ABOVE: General William Hardee led the corps that mounted the Confederate attack on the Union right wing (Sherman) on the first day of the battle.

ter of our tents during the rain, and also to get away from the shells that were dropped upon them by the gunboats every fifteen minutes during the night.

The position of the Union troops on the morning of the 7th was as follows: General Lew. Wallace on the right; Sherman on his left; then McClernand and then Hurlbut. Nelson, of Buell's army, was on our extreme left, next to the river. Crittenden was next in line after Nelson and on his right; McCook followed and formed the extreme right of Buell's command. My old command thus formed the right wing, while the troops directly under Buell constituted the left wing of the army. These relative positions were retained during the entire day, or until the enemy was driven from the field.

In a very short time the battle became general all along the line. This day everything was favorable to the Union side. We had now become the attacking party. The enemy was driven back all day, as we had been the day before, until finally he beat a precipitate retreat. The last point held by him was near the road leading from the landing to Corinth, on the left of Sherman and right of McClernand. About three o'clock, being near that point and seeing that the enemy was giving way everywhere else, I gathered up a couple of regiments, or parts of regiments, from troops near by, formed them in line of battle and marched them forward, going in front myself to prevent premature or long-range firing. At this point there was a clearing between us and the enemy favorable for charging, although exposed. I knew the enemy were ready to break and only wanted a little encouragement from us to go quickly and join their friends who had started earlier. After marching to within musket-range I stopped and let the troops pass. The command, *Charge*, was given, and was executed with loud cheers and with a run; when the last of the enemy broke.

*   *   *

Shiloh was the severest battle fought at the West during the war, and but few in the East equalled it for hard, determined fight-ing. I saw an open field, in our possession on the second day, over which the Confederates had made repeated charges the day before, so covered with dead that it would have been possible to walk across the clearing, in any direction, stepping on dead bodies, without a foot touching the ground. On our side National and Confederate troops were mingled together in about equal proportions; but on the remainder of the field nearly all were Confederates. On one

ABOVE: Union troops under General Rousseau's command recapture artillery that the Confederates had taken from them earlier in the battle.

LEFT: Kentucky-bred Unionist Lovell H. Rousseau fought with distinction at Shiloh and elsewhere. He stayed in the army after the war and rose to the permanent rank of brigadier general.

ABOVE: A patriotic engraving shows Grant leading an heroic charge at Shiloh. It does not much matter that the officer in question looks little like Grant, since there was never any such charge.

part, which had evidently not been ploughed for several years, probably because the land was poor, bushes had grown up, some to the height of eight or ten feet. There was not one of these left standing unpierced by bullets. The smaller ones were all cut down.

Contrary to all my experience up to that time, and to the experience of the army I was then commanding, we were on the defensive. We were without intrenchments or defensive advantages of any sort, and more than half the army engaged the first day was without experience or even drill as soldiers. The officers with them, except the division commanders and possibly two or three of the brigade commanders, were equally inexperienced in war. The result was a Union victory that gave the men who achieved it great confidence in themselves ever after.

The enemy fought bravely, but they had started out to defeat and destroy an army and capture a position. They failed in both, with very heavy loss in killed and wounded, and must have gone back discouraged and convinced that the "Yankee" was not an enemy to be despised. . . .

General Albert Sidney Johnston, who commanded the Confederate forces at the beginning of the battle, was disabled by a wound on the afternoon of the first day. This wound, as I understood afterwards, was not necessarily fatal, or even dangerous. But he was a man who would not abandon what he deemed an important trust in the face of danger and consequently continued in the saddle, commanding, until so exhausted by the loss of blood that he had to be taken from his horse, and soon after died. The

LEFT: Confederate dead await burial. Shiloh, with combined casualties of around 24,000, was easily the most bloody battle so far fought in the Western Hemisphere.

RIGHT: When Albert Sidney Johnston received a mortal wound at Shiloh many in the South believed that the CSA had lost its greatest general. Grant, however, was never much impressed by the tactics that Johnston used at Shiloh.

news was not long in reaching our side and I suppose was quite an encouragement to the National soldiers.

I had known Johnston slightly in the Mexican war and later as an officer in the regular army. He was a man of high character and ability. His contemporaries at West Point, and officers generally who came to know him personally later and who remained on our side, expected him to prove the most formidable man to meet that the Confederacy would produce.

I once wrote that nothing occurred in his brief command of an army to prove or disprove the high estimate that had been placed upon his military ability; but after studying the orders and dispatches of Johnston I am compelled to materially modify my views of that officer's qualifications as a soldier. My judgment is now that he was vacillating and undecided in his actions. . . .

He knew the National troops were preparing to attack him in his chosen position. But he had evidently become so disturbed at the results of his operations that he resolved to strike out in an offensive campaign which would restore all that was lost, and if successful accomplish still more. . . . The design was a bold one; but . . . in the execution Johnston showed vacillation and indecision. He left Corinth on the 2d of April and was not ready to attack until the 6th. The distance his army had to march was less than twenty miles. [General P. G. T.] Beauregard, his second in command, was opposed to the attack for two reasons: first, he thought, if let alone the National troops would attack the Confederates in their intrenchments; second, we were in ground of our own choosing and would necessarily be intrenched. Johnston not only listened to the objection of Beauregard to an attack, but held a council of war on the subject on the morning of the 5th. On the evening of the same day he was in consultation with some of his generals on the same subject, and still again on the morning of the 6th. During this last consultation, and before a decision had been reached, the battle began by the National troops opening fire on the enemy. This seemed to settle the question as to whether there was to be any battle of Shiloh. It also seems to me to settle the question as to whether there was a surprise.

I do not question the personal courage of General Johnston, or his ability. But he did not win the distinction predicted for him by many of his friends. He did prove that as a general he was over-estimated.

General Beauregard was next in rank to Johnston and succeeded to the command, which he retained to the close of the battle and during the subsequent retreat on Corinth, as well as in the siege of that place. His tactics have been severely criticised by Confederate writers, but I do not believe his fallen chief could have done any better under the circumstances. Some of these critics claim that Shiloh was won when Johnston fell, and that if he had not fallen the army under me would have been annihilated or captured. *Ifs* defeated the Confederates at Shiloh. There is little doubt that we would have been disgracefully beaten *if* all the shells and bullets fired by us had passed harmlessly over the enemy and *if* all of theirs had taken effect. Commanding generals are liable to be killed during engagements; and the fact that when he was shot Johnston was leading a brigade to induce it to make a charge which had been repeatedly ordered, is evidence that there was neither the universal demoralization on our side nor the unbounded confidence on theirs which has been claimed. . . .

The endeavor of the enemy on the first day was simply to hurl their men against ours — first at one point, then at another, some-

times at several points at once. This they did with daring and energy, until at night the rebel troops were worn out. Our effort during the same time was to be prepared to resist assaults wherever made. The object of the Confederates on the second day was to get away with as much of their army and material as possible. Ours then was to drive them from our front, and to capture or destroy as great a part as possible of their men and material. We were successful in driving them back, but not so successful in captures as if farther pursuit could have been made. As it was, we captured or recaptured on the second day about as much artillery as we lost on the first; and, leaving out the one great capture of Prentiss, we took more prisoners on Monday than the enemy gained from us on Sunday. . . .

Our loss in the two days' fight was 1,754 killed, 8,408 wounded and 2,885 missing. Of these, 2,103 were in the Army of the Ohio. Beauregard reported a total loss of 10,699, of whom 1,728 were killed, 8,012 wounded and 957 missing. This estimate must be incorrect. We buried, by actual count, more of the

BELOW: William Bate was still serving as an enlisted man in a Tennessee regiment when he was wounded at Shiloh. By the war's end he would be a Confederate major general.

RIGHT: P.G.T. Beauregard, Johnston's second-in-command, was already famous for his contributions to the CSA's victories at Fort Sumter and First Manassas. When Johnston was wounded on the first day at Shiloh, Beauregard took his place, only to lose the battle the next day.

BELOW: John C. Breckinridge commanded the Confederate corps that would cover the Southern retreat at the end of the second day's fighting at the Battle of Shiloh.

enemy's dead in front of the divisions of McClernand and Sherman alone than here reported, and 4,000 was the estimate of the burial parties for the whole field. Beauregard reports the Confederate force on the 6th at over 40,000, and their total loss during the two days at 10,699; and at the same time declares that he could put only 20,000 men in battle on the morning of the 7th. . . .

Up to the battle of Shiloh I, as well as thousands of other citizens, believed that the rebellion against the Government would collapse suddenly and soon, if a decisive victory could be gained over any of its armies. Donelson and Henry were such victories. . . . But when Confederate armies were collected which not only attempted to hold a line farther south, from Memphis to Chattanooga, Knoxville and on to the Atlantic, but assumed the offensive and made such a gallant effort to regain what had been lost, then, indeed, I gave up all idea of saving the Union except by complete conquest. . . .

FAR LEFT: From his vantage point on the limb of a tree a Confederate sharpshooter takes aim at an enemy.

LEFT: A typically-equipped Confederate infantryman.

LEFT: Leonidas Polk, who led one of the four Confederate corps that fought at Shiloh, was an Episcopalian bishop. Though a West Point graduate, he had never served in the field before Jefferson Davis gave him a major generalcy in 1861. In practice, he proved to be a mediocre commander.

Chapter III

Vicksburg

Shiloh was unquestionably a Union victory, but because Grant's exhausted forces failed to pursue the retreating enemy aggressively enough Shiloh remained an unexploited victory. Those among Grant's equals and superiors who were inclined to be critical of him (Henry Halleck among them) harped on this and on the fact that Grant had allowed himself to be surprised by the enemy. But Abraham Lincoln had been impressed by how hard – and ultimately successfully – Grant had fought, and could not help contrasting this to the ponderous, excessively cautious conduct of the campaign that Union General George McClellan was then mounting on the Virginia peninsula. "I can't spare this man," said Lincoln of Grant. "He fights." And certainly the fact that McClellan's Peninsular Campaign soon turned into a debacle (to be followed by a whole string of Eastern disasters at Second Manassas, Fredericksburg, and Chancellorsville) did nothing to change Lincoln's opinion of this rising star in his Western armies.

Lincoln's support no doubt helped Grant, but it did not altogether save him from his critics. After Shiloh, Halleck assumed direct field command of the Western armies, in effect kicking Grant upstairs by giving him a more-or-less ceremonial posting as second-in-command. By April 29, 1862, Halleck was ready to move on Corinth. Incredibly, it took him until May 25 to get there, and then, instead of attacking the city, he besieged it. Of this period

BELOW: President Lincoln with his cabinet. Though Halleck and some other senior Union army officers were inclined to belittle Grant's victory at Shiloh, the President was impressed, a fact that did much for Grant's career.

ABOVE: The Battle of Corinth, fought on October 3-4, 1862. Grant's successful defense of Corinth was a considerable strategic victory, but Grant was nevertheless critical of his principal commander in the field, William Rosecrans, for not pursuing the fleeing enemy more aggressively.

LEFT: An encampment of the Union army outside Corinth during Halleck's siege of the city in May 1862. Grant was disgusted by Halleck's lack of enterprise in choosing to besiege rather than attack.

OPPOSITE RIGHT: David Glasgow Farragut, greatest Federal naval commander of the Civil War, played a crucial role in opening the Mississippi to Union control when, in April 1862, he daringly ran past powerful Confederate river forts to capture the key port city of New Orleans.

OPPOSITE LEFT: Earl Van Dorn was one of the more luckless Confederate generals. Though he had some minor successes as a raider, he lost both of the major battles – Pea Ridge and Corinth – in which he was in command. He was killed by a jealous husband in 1863.

BELOW: Union batteries repel the attacking Confederate forces of Earl Van Dorn at Corinth on October 4, 1862.

Grant wrote: "For myself I was little more than an observer. . . . My position was so embarrassing in fact that I made several applications during the siege to be relieved."

P. G. T. Beauregard, who commanded the Confederate forces in Corinth, could see no point in allowing himself to be starved into submission, and on the night of May 29-30 he evacuated the city. Halleck did not pursue him. "The possession of Corinth by the National troops was of strategic importance," wrote Grant, "but the victory was barren in every other particular." Nevertheless, on July 11 a grateful Washington recalled Halleck to the capital to make him general-in-chief of all the Union armies. His departure ended Grant's purgatory, leaving him de facto command of District of Tennessee (he would be formally named to that post only in October).

The Union armies that Halleck had concentrated around Corinth began to disperse soon after his departure for Washington, and Confederate forces accordingly began to gather for the reconquest of Corinth and southern Tennessee. The assault on Corinth, led by Confederate General Earl Van Dorn, began on October 3. A fierce two-day battle followed, but Grant's troops eventually routed the attackers. "The battle," said Grant, "relieved me of any further anxiety for the safety of the territory within my jurisdiction, and soon after receiving reinforcements I suggested to the general-in-chief a forward movement against Vicksburg." Halleck approved the proposal.

The Confederate fortress-city of Vicksburg, Mississippi, was indeed now the key to Union victory in the West – and perhaps in the East as well. Union grand strategy was heavily predicated on gaining control of the entire Mississippi River, thus bisecting the greater South along a north-south axis. If this could be done, the Union could then concentrate on trying to bisect the Old South along an east-west axis, most likely via a drive east through Georgia to the sea. By the autumn of 1862 eventual Federal conquest of the Mississippi had become a real possibility. Ever since April, when U.S. Admiral David Farragut had captured New Orleans, Union land and naval forces along the river had gradually extended the area under their control until Confederate holdings were effectively reduced to that (considerable) stretch of the left bank that lay between Port Hudson, Louisiana, and Vicksburg. Yet Vicksburg would prove to be a singularly tough nut to crack, as Grant's Memoirs make all too clear.

Vicksburg was important to the enemy because it occupied the first high ground coming close to the river below Memphis. From there a railroad runs east, connecting with other roads leading to all points of the Southern States. A railroad also starts from the opposite side of the river, extending west as far as Shreveport, Louisiana. Vicksburg was the only channel, at the time of the events of which this chapter treats, connecting the parts of the Confederacy divided by the Mississippi. So long as it was held by the enemy, the free navigation of the river was prevented. Hence its importance. Points on the river between Vicksburg and Port Hudson were held as dependencies; but their fall was sure to follow the capture of the former place.

The campaign against Vicksburg commenced on the 2d of November as indicated in a dispatch to the general-in-chief in the following words: "I have commenced a movement on Grand Junction, with three divisions from Corinth and two from Bolivar. Will leave here [Jackson, Tennessee] tomorrow, and take command in person. If found practicable, I will go to Holly Springs, and, may be, Grenada, completing railroad and telegraph as I go."

At this time my command was holding the Mobile and Ohio railroad from about twenty-five miles south of Corinth, north to Columbus, Kentucky; the Mississippi Central from Bolivar north to its junction with the Mobile

and Ohio; the Memphis and Charleston from Corinth east to Bear Creek, and the Mississippi River from Cairo to Memphis. My entire command was no more than was necessary to hold these lines, and hardly that if kept on the defensive. By moving against the enemy and into his unsubdued, or not yet captured, territory, driving their army before us, these lines would nearly hold them-selves; thus affording a large force for field operations. My moving force at that time was about 30,000 men, and I estimated the enemy confronting me, under [General John C.] Pemberton, at about the same number. General [James] McPherson commanded my left wing and General C. S. Hamilton the centre, while [General William T.] Sherman was at Memphis with the right

wing. Pemberton was fortified at the Talla-hatchie, but occupied Holly Springs and Grand Junction on the Mississippi Central railroad. On the 8th we occupied Grand Junction and La Grange, throwing a considerable force seven or eight miles south, along the line of the railroad. The road from Bolivar forward was repaired and put in running order as the troops advanced. . . .

Grant had hoped that the lure of frustrating the deliberate Union advance on Vicksburg might induce Pemberton to move his forces far enough north of the city so that Sherman could get in behind them and cut them off. But it was not to be: by mid-December Pemberton had safely withdrawn behind Vicksburg's formidable defenses

LEFT: The most famous of the very powerful defenses that made Vicksburg impregnable from any attack from the west was "Whistling Dick," a big 18-pounder that was so-named because the rifling in its barrel imparted a peculiar spin to cannonballs, causing them to emit an eerie high-pitched noise when in flight. "Whistling Dick" would send the Union gunboat *Cincinnati* to the bottom while Grant was besieging Vicksburg in 1863.

before Sherman could engage him. Grant suffered another, smaller vexation when John A. McClernand, one of his "political generals," persuaded his political sponsors in Washington to let him undertake a brief detached (and, as it happened, successful) campaign against Confederate Fort Hindman on the Arkansas River, thus weakening Grant's army at just the time it was assembling before Vicksburg. But by the end of January 1863 Grant had gotten Halleck to order the insubordinate McClernand to place himself completely under Grant's authority, and the real work on the Vicksburg campaign could begin. From his new headquarters at Young's Point, Louisiana, a little upriver from Vicksburg, Grant pondered the difficulties that lay before him.

ABOVE RIGHT: In command of the big Vicksburg garrison was Confederate General John C. Pemberton, yet another of Grant's former comrades-in-arms from pre-Civil War days. Grant's personal knowledge of Pemberton's character and abilities would serve Grant well in the coming campaign.

RIGHT: Union General John A. McClernand was easily the most troublesome of Grant's lieutenants in 1862-63. A "political general," he was ambitious, often insubordinate, and not overly effective in the field. Grant's dislike of him is made all too clear in the *Memoirs*.

It was in January the troops took their position opposite Vicksburg. The water was very high and the rains were incessant. There seemed no possibility of a land movement before the end of March or later, and it would not do to lie idle all this time. The effect would be demoralizing to the troops and injurious to their health. Friends in the North would have grown more and more discouraged, and enemies in the same section more and more insolent in their gibes and denunciation of the cause and those engaged in it. . . .

Vicksburg, as stated before, is on the first high land coming to the river's edge, below that on which Memphis stands. The bluff, or high land, follows the left bank of the Yazoo for some distance and continues in a southerly direction to the Mississippi River, thence it runs along the Mississippi to Warrenton, six miles below. The Yazoo River leaves the high land a short distance below Haines' Bluff and empties into the Mississippi nine miles above Vicksburg. Vicksburg is built on this high land where the Mississippi washes the base of the hill. Haines' Bluff, eleven miles from Vicksburg, on the

Yazoo River, was strongly fortified. The whole distance from there to Vicksburg and thence to Warrenton was also intrenched, with batteries at suitable distances and rifle-pits connecting them.

From Young's Point the Mississippi turns in a north-easterly direction to a point just above the city, when it again turns and runs south-westerly, leaving vessels, which might attempt to run the blockade, exposed to the fire of batteries six miles below the city before they were in range of the upper batteries. Since then the river has made a cut-off, leaving what was the peninsula in front of the city, an island. North of the Yazoo was all a marsh, heavily timbered, cut up with bayous, and much overflowed. A front attack was therefore impossible, and was never contemplated; certainly not by me. The problem then became, how to secure a landing on high ground east of the Mississippi without an apparent retreat. Then commenced a series of experiments to consume time, and to divert the attention of the enemy, of my troops and of the public generally. I, myself, never felt great confidence that any of the experiments resorted

BELOW: A view of Vicksburg from the Mississippi River. The bluff rising behind the riverfront was dotted with batteries, making attack from the river almost unthinkable. The land to the north of the city was swampy and nearly impassable, and that to the south not much better and heavily defended. Thus the only good military avenue to Vicksburg was from the east, *ie.*, from *inside* territory held by the enemy.

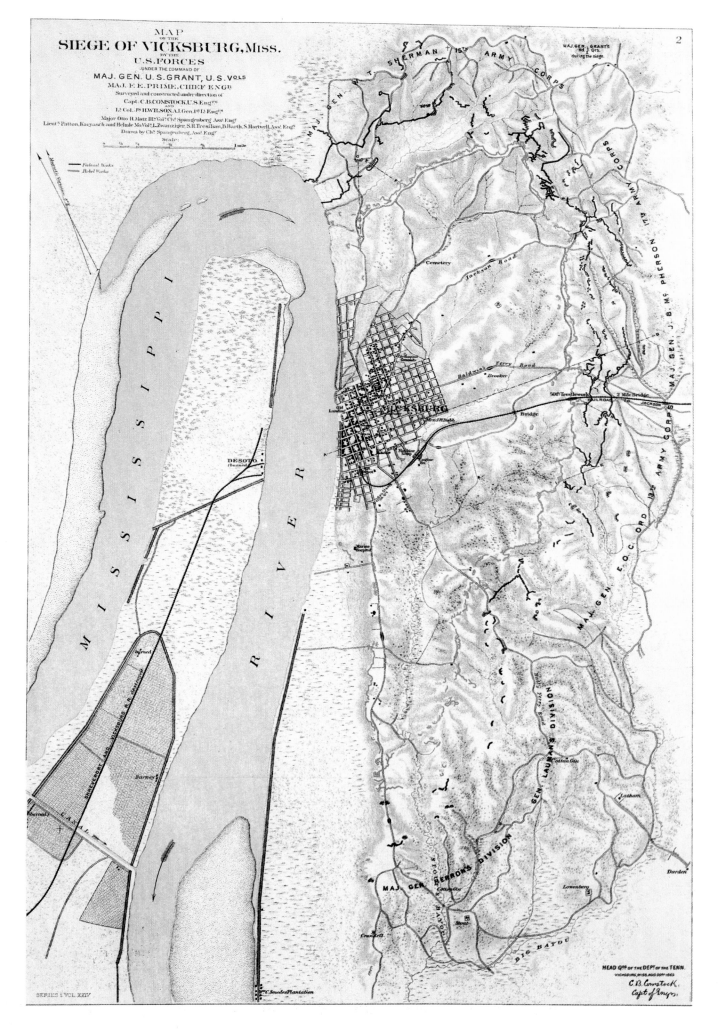

to would prove successful. Nevertheless I was always prepared to take advantage of them in case they did.

In 1862 General Thomas Williams had come up from New Orleans and cut a ditch ten or twelve feet wide and about as deep, straight across from Young's Point to the river below. The distance across was a little over a mile. It was Williams' expectation that when the river rose it would cut a navigable channel through; but the canal started in an eddy from both ends, and, of course, it only filled up with water on the rise without doing any execution in the way of cutting. Mr. Lincoln had navigated the Mississippi in his younger days and understood well its tendency to change its channel, in places, from time to time. He set much store accordingly by this canal. General McClernand had been, therefore, directed before I went to Young's Point to push the work of widening and deepening this canal. After my arrival the work was diligently pushed with about 4,000 men – as many as could be used to advantage – until interrupted by a sudden rise in the river that broke a dam at the upper end, which had been put there to keep the water out until the excavation was completed. This was on the 8th of March.

Even if the canal had proven a success, so far as to be navigable for steamers, it could not have been of much advantage to us. It runs in a direction almost perpendicular to the line of bluffs on the opposite side, or east bank, of the river. As soon as the enemy discovered what we were doing he established a battery commanding the canal throughout its length. This battery soon drove out our dredges, two in number, which were doing the work of thousands of men. Had the canal been completed it might have proven of some use in running transports through, under the cover of night, to use below; but they would yet have to run batteries, though for a much shorter distance.

While this work was progressing we were busy in other directions, trying to find an available landing on high ground on the east bank of the river, or to make water-ways to get below the city, avoiding the batteries. . . .

Another expedient that was tried that winter involved trying to open a canal to Lake Providence, from which Federal gunboats might, by following a somewhat tortuous route through rivers and bayous, re-enter the Mississippi south of Vicksburg. It was eventually abandoned in favor of two efforts to cut across the Yazoo delta, first via

OPPOSITE: A Union army map showing Vicksburg and its environs at the time of the siege. Virtually the whole outer ring of Confederate defenses was sited high on commanding bluffs.

BELOW: A view from Vicksburg looking northwest toward the hairpin bend of the river.

ABOVE: Central Vicksburg. The town was fairly large and prosperous, but it still had something of a frontier look about it in 1862.

OPPOSITE TOP: Union General Francis Blair (center) with his staff. One of Sherman's better division commanders, he would have the misfortune to be temporarily attached to McClernand's do-nothing corps in the critical Battle of Champion's Hill.

OPPOSITE BOTTOM: General G.W. Morgan led a division in the failed Union effort to take the Chickasaw Bluffs on the Yazoo, north of Vicksburg, in December 1862. Such early setbacks convinced Grant that there could be no easy solution to the problem of how to capture Vicksburg.

the so-called Yazoo Pass Route and then via the Steel's Bayou Route. Both projects failed. By March, when the fairweather campaigning season was at hand, it seemed clear that the only way Admiral David Dixon Porter's riverine squadron would ever get south of Vicksburg would be sailing directly under the guns of the city's massive batteries. The risks were appalling, but they had to be faced, for Grant had concluded that his only hope now lay in ferrying his army across the river and attacking Vicksburg from the east, from inside *enemy territory.*

I had had in contemplation the whole winter the movement by land to a point below Vicksburg from which to operate, subject only to the possible but not expected success of some one of the expedients resorted to for the purpose of giving us a different base. This could not be undertaken until the waters receded. I did not therefore communicate this plan, even to an officer of my staff, until it was necessary to make preparations for the start. My recollection is that

Admiral Porter was the first one to whom I mentioned it. The co-operation of the navy was absolutely essential to the success (even to the contemplation) of such an enterprise. I had no more authority to command Porter than he had to command me. It was necessary to have part of his fleet below Vicksburg if the troops went there. Steamers to use as ferries were also essential. The navy was the only escort and protection for these steamers, all of which in getting below had to run about fourteen miles of batteries. Porter fell into the plan at once, and suggested that he had better superintend the preparation of the steamers selected to run the batteries, as sailors would probably understand the work better than soldiers. I was glad to accept his proposition, not only because I admitted his argument, but because it would enable me to keep from the enemy a little longer our designs. Porter's fleet was on the east side of the river above the mouth of the Yazoo, entirely concealed from the enemy by the dense forests that intervened. Even spies could not get near him, on account of the undergrowth and overflowed lands. Suspicions of some

mysterious movements were aroused. Our river guards discovered one day a small skiff moving quietly and mysteriously up the river near the east shore, from the direction of Vicksburg, towards the fleet. On overhauling the boat they found a small white flag, not much larger than a handkerchief, set up in the stern, no doubt intended as a flag of truce in case of discovery. The boat, crew and passengers were brought ashore to me. The chief personage aboard proved to be Jacob Thompson, Secretary of the Interior under the administration of President Buchanan. After a pleasant conversation of half an hour or more I allowed the boat and crew, passengers and all, to return to Vicksburg, without creating a suspicion that there was a doubt in my mind as to the good faith of Mr. Thompson and his flag.

Admiral Porter proceeded with the preparation of the steamers for their hazardous passage of the enemy's batteries. The great essential was to protect the boilers from the enemy's shot, and to conceal the fires under the boilers from view. This he accomplished by loading the steamers, between the guards and boilers on the boiler deck up to the deck

ABOVE: Flag Officer David Dixon Porter's Mississippi Squadron makes its daring run past the big guns of the Vicksburg batteries on the night of April 16, 1863. The ships were under heavy fire for over two hours, but only one, a transport, was lost.

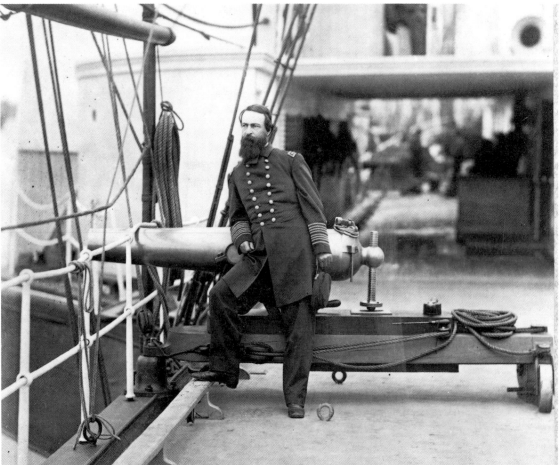

RIGHT: David Dixon Porter. For his contribution to the success of Grant's Vicksburg Campaign, Porter was rewarded by a promotion that jumped him two grades in permanent rank to a rear admiralcy.

above, with bales of hay and cotton, and the deck in front of the boilers in the same way, adding sacks of grain. The hay and grain would be wanted below, and could not be transported in sufficient quantity by the muddy roads over which we expected to march.

Before this I had been collecting, from St. Louis and Chicago, yawls and barges to be used as ferries when we got below. By the 16th of April Porter was ready to start on his perilous trip. The advance, flagship *Benton*, Porter commanding, started at ten o'clock at night, followed at intervals of a few minutes by the *Lafayette* with a captured steamer, the *Price*, lashed to her side, the *Louisville, Mound City, Pittsburgh* and *Carondelet* – all of these being naval vessels. Next came the transports – *Forest Queen, Silver Wave* and *Henry Clay*, each towing barges loaded with coal to be used as fuel by the naval and transport steamers when below the batteries. The gunboat *Tuscumbia* brought up the rear. Soon after the start a battery between Vicksburg and Warrenton opened fire across the intervening peninsula, followed by the upper batteries, and then by batteries all along the line. The gunboats ran up close under the bluffs, delivering their fire in return at short distances, probably without much effect. They were under fire for more than two hours and every vessel was struck many times, but with little damage to the gunboats. The transports did not fare so well. The *Henry Clay* was disabled and deserted by her crew. Soon after a shell burst in the cotton packed about the boilers, set the vessel on fire and burned her to the water's edge. The burning mass, however, floated down to Carthage before grounding, as did also one of the barges in tow.

The enemy were evidently expecting our fleet, for they were ready to light up the river by means of bonfires on the east side and by firing houses on the point of land opposite the city on the Louisiana side. The sight was magnificent, but terrible. I witnessed it from the deck of a river transport, run out into the middle of the river and as low down as it was prudent to go. My mind was much relieved when I learned that no one on the transports had been killed and but few, if any, wounded. During the running of the batteries men were stationed in the holds of the transports to partially stop with cotton shot-holes that might be made in the hulls. All damage was afterwards soon repaired under the direction of Admiral Porter. . . .

Once Porter's squadron was below Vicksburg, Grant set his army in motion. While Sherman made a demonstration north of Vicksburg, McClernand's and McPherson's corps moved south along the Louisiana shore, sometimes marching and sometimes ferried in Porter's transports, until they reached a point a little south of the Confederate stronghold Grand Gulf.

When the troops debarked, the evening of the 29th, it was expected that we would have to go to Rodney, about nine miles below, to find a landing; but that night a colored man came in who informed me that a good landing would be found at Bruinsburg, a few miles above Rodney, from which point there was a good road leading to Port Gibson some twelve miles in the interior. The information was found correct, and our landing was effected without opposition.

Sherman had not left his position above Vicksburg yet. On the morning of the 27th I ordered him to create a diversion by moving his corps up the Yazoo and threatening an attack on Haines' Bluff.

My object was to compel Pemberton to keep as much force about Vicksburg as I could, until I could secure a good footing on high land east of the river. The move was eminently successful and, as we afterwards learned, created great confusion about Vicksburg and doubts about our real design. Sherman moved the day of our attack on Grand Gulf, the 29th, with ten regiments of his command and eight gunboats which Porter had left above Vicksburg.

He debarked his troops and apparently

BELOW: River steamers unload supplies at Young's Point, Grant's headquarters above Vicksburg, in March 1863.

ABOVE: The Confederates had no monopoly on artillery in the Vicksburg Campaign. Here, a Union battery composed of mixed siege and field guns.

OPPOSITE TOP: Some of the larger houses in Vicksburg. The house in the foreground would be taken over by the U.S. Army Signal Corps after the city's capture.

OPPOSITE BOTTOM: General John A. Logan (fifth from right) was an excellent divisional commander in McPherson's corps. He was given a corps command of his own at the end of the Vicksburg Campaign.

made every preparation to attack the enemy while the navy bombarded the main forts at Haines' Bluff. This move was made without a single casualty in either branch of the service. On the first of May Sherman received orders from me (sent from Hard Times the evening of the 29th of April) to withdraw from the front of Haines' Bluff and follow McPherson with two divisions as fast as he could.

I had established a depot of supplies at Perkins' plantation. Now that all our gunboats were below Grand Gulf it was possible that the enemy might fit out boats in the Big Black with improvised armament and attempt to destroy these supplies. McPherson was at Hard Times with a portion of his corps, and the depot was protected by a part of his command. The night of the 29th I directed him to arm one of the transports with artillery and send it up to Perkins' plantation as a guard; and also to have the siege guns we had brought along moved there and put in position.

The embarkation below Grand Gulf took place at De Shroon's, Louisiana, six miles above Bruinsburg, Mississippi. Early on the morning of 30th of April McClernand's corps

and one division of McPherson's corps were speedily landed.

When this was effected I felt a degree of relief scarcely ever equalled since. Vicksburg was not yet taken it is true, nor were its defenders demoralized by any of our previous moves. I was now in the enemy's country, with a vast river and the stronghold of Vicksburg between me and my base of supplies. But I was on dry ground on the same side of the river with the enemy. All the campaigns, labors, hardships and exposures from the month of December previous to this time that had been made and endured, were for . . . this one object.

I had with me the 13th corps, General McClernand commanding, and two brigades of [John A.] Logan's division of the 17th corps, General McPherson commanding – in all not more than twenty thousand men to commence the campaign with. These were soon reinforced by the remaining brigade of Logan's division and [M.M.] Crocker's division of the 17th corps. On the 7th of May I was further reinforced by Sherman with two divisions of his, the 15th corps. My total force was then about thirty-three thousand men.

The enemy occupied Grand Gulf, Haines' Bluff and Jackson with a force of nearly sixty thousand men. Jackson is fifty miles east of Vicksburg and is connected with it by a railroad. My first problem was to capture Grand Gulf to use as a base. . . .

The key to the taking of Grand Gulf was the capture of strategically-located Port Gibson, 12 miles inland. Both the Grand Gulf garrison and Grant's troops raced toward Port Gibson, clashed there, and the Union prevailed. During the night of May 2 the Confederates evacuated Grand Gulf.

When I reached Grand Gulf May 3rd I had not been with my baggage since the 27th of April and consequently had had no change of underclothing, no meal except such as I could pick up sometimes at other head-quarters, and no tent to cover me. The first thing I did was to get a bath, borrow some fresh underclothing from one of the naval officers and get a good meal on the flagship. Then I wrote letters to the general-in-chief informing him of our present position, dispatches to be telegraphed from Cairo, orders to General [J. C.] Sullivan commanding above Vicksburg, and gave orders to all my corps commanders. About twelve o'clock at night I was through my work and

started for Hankinson's ferry, arriving there before daylight. While at Grand Gulf I heard from [Nathaniel] Banks, who was on the Red River, and who said that he could not be at Port Hudson before the 10th of May and then with only 15,000 men. Up to this time my intention had been to secure Grand Gulf, as a base of supplies, detach McClernand's corps to Banks and co-operate with him in the reduction of Port Hudson.

The news from Banks forced upon me a different plan of campaign from the one intended. To wait for his co-operation would have detained me at least a month. The reinforcements would not have reached ten thousand men after deducting casualties and necessary river guards at all high points close to the river for over three hundred miles. The enemy would have strengthened his position and been reinforced by more men than Banks could have brought. I therefore determined to move independently of Banks, cut loose from my base, destroy the rebel force in rear of Vicksburg and invest or capture the city.

Grand Gulf was accordingly given up as a base and the authorities at Washington were notified. I knew well that Halleck's caution would lead him to disapprove of this course; but it was the only one that gave any chance of success. The time it would take to communicate with Washington and get a reply would be so great that I could not be interfered with until it was demonstrated whether my plan was practicable. Even Sherman, who afterwards ignored bases of supplies other than what were afforded by the country while marching through four States of the Confederacy with an army more than twice as large as mine at this time, wrote me from Hankinson's ferry, advising me of the impossibility of supplying our army over a single road. He urged me to "stop all troops till your army is partially supplied with wagons, and then act as quick as possible; for this road will be jammed, as sure as life." To this I replied: "I do not calculate upon the possibility of supplying the army with full rations from Grand Gulf. I know it will be impossible without constructing additional roads. What I do expect is to get up what rations of hard bread, coffee and salt we can, and make the country furnish the balance." . . .

Up to this point our movements had been made without serious opposition. My line was now nearly parallel with the Jackson and Vicksburg railroad and about seven

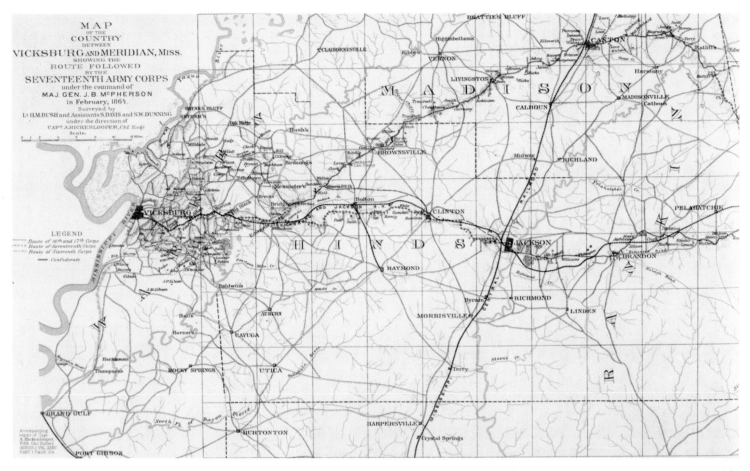

miles south of it. The right was at Raymond eighteen miles from Jackson, McPherson commanding; Sherman was in the centre on Fourteen Mile Creek, his advance thrown across; McClernand to the left, also on Fourteen Mile Creek, advance across, and his pickets within two miles of Edward's station, where the enemy had concentrated a considerable force and where they undoubtedly expected us to attack. McClernand's left was on the Big Black. In all our moves, up to this time, the left had hugged the Big Black closely, and all the ferries had been guarded to prevent the enemy throwing a force on our rear.

McPherson encountered the enemy, five thousand strong with two batteries under General [J.] Gregg, about two miles out of Raymond. This was about two P.M. Logan was in advance with one of his brigades. He deployed and moved up to engage the enemy. McPherson ordered the road in rear to be cleared of wagons, and the balance of Logan's division, and Crocker's, which was still farther in rear, to come forward with all dispatch. The order was obeyed with alacrity. Logan got his division in position for assault before Crocker could get up, and attacked with vigor, carrying the enemy's position easily, sending Gregg flying from the field not to appear against our front

again until we met at Jackson.

In this battle McPherson lost 66 killed, 339 wounded, and 37 missing – nearly or not quite all from Logan's division. The enemy's loss was 100 killed, 305 wounded, besides 415 taken prisoners. . . .

When the news reached me of McPherson's victory at Raymond about sundown my position was with Sherman. I decided at once to turn the whole column towards Jackson and capture that place without delay.

Pemberton was now on my left, with, as I supposed, about 18,000 men; in fact, as I learned afterwards, with nearly 50,000. A force was also collecting on my right, at Jackson, the point where all the railroads communicating with Vicksburg connect. All the enemy's supplies of men and stores would come by that point. As I hoped in the end to besiege Vicksburg, I must first destroy all possibility of aid. I therefore determined to move swiftly towards Jackson, destroy or drive any force in that direction and then turn upon Pemberton. But by moving against Jackson, I uncovered my own communication. So I finally decided to have none – to cut loose altogether from my base and move my whole force eastward. I then had no fears for my communications, and if I moved quickly enough could turn upon Pemberton before he could attack me in the rear. . . .

General Joseph E. Johnston arrived at Jackson in the night of the 13th from Tennessee, and immediately assumed command of all the Confederate troops in Mississippi. I knew he was expecting reinforcements from the south and east. . . .

I notified General Halleck that I should attack the State capital on the 14th. A courier carried the dispatch to Grand Gulf through an unprotected country.

Sherman and McPherson communicated with each other during the night and arranged to reach Jackson at about the same hour. It rained in torrents during the night of the 13th and the fore part of the day of the 14th. The roads were intolerable, and in some places on Sherman's line, where the land was low, they were covered more than a foot deep with water. But the troops never murmured. By nine o'clock Crocker, of McPherson's corps, who was now in advance, came upon the enemy's pickets and speedily drove them in upon the main body. They were outside of the intrenchments in a strong position, and proved to be

the troops that had been driven out of Raymond. Johnston had been reinforced during the night by Georgia and South Carolina regiments, so that his force amounted to eleven thousand men, and he was expecting still more.

Sherman also came upon the rebel pickets some distance out from the town, but speedily drove them in. He was now on the south and south-west of Jackson confronting the Confederates behind their breastworks, while McPherson's right was nearly two miles north, occupying a line running north and south across the Vicksburg railroad. Artillery was brought up and reconnoissances made preparatory to an assault. McPherson brought up Logan's division while he deployed Crocker's for the assault. Sherman made similar dispositions on the right. By eleven A.M. both were ready to attack. . . .

I slept that night in the room that Johnston occupied the night before. . . .

On the night of the 13th Johnston had sent the following dispatch to Pemberton at Edward's station: "I have lately arrived, and learn that Major-General Sherman is between us with four divisions at Clinton. It is important to establish communication, that you may be reinforced. If practicable, come up in his rear at once. To beat such a detachment would be of immense value. All the troops you can quickly assemble should be brought. Time is all-important." This dispatch was sent in triplicate, by different messengers. One of the messengers happened to be a loyal man who had been expelled from Memphis some months before by Hurlbut for uttering disloyal and threatening sentiments. There was a good deal of parade about his expulsion, ostensibly as a warning to those who entertained the sentiments he expressed; but Hurlbut and the expelled man understood each other. He delivered his copy of Johnston's dispatch to McPherson who forwarded it to me.

ABOVE: Sherman with some of the generals who accompanied him on the historic Georgia and Carolinas campaigns of 1864-65. Long before anyone else, Grant recognized in his premier lieutenant the spark of true military genius.

OPPOSITE TOP: Grant's foes in the Vicksburg Campaign were not to be taken lightly. The Confederacy could offer few generals more talented than Joseph E. Johnston.

OPPOSITE BOTTOM: One of the many minor players in the Vicksburg drama, W.T. Clark was adjutant general on James McPherson's staff. He later became a hated carpetbagger.

RIGHT: General William T. Sherman. This great general is as controversial today as he was in his own time. His admirers have always hailed him as a genius who had an uncanny grasp of how warfare was changing in the modern era. His critics have always thought him an unchivalrous and callous brute. Grant's admiration for Sherman as a commander was unqualified, surpassed only by Sherman's admiration for Grant.

Receiving this dispatch on the 14th I ordered McPherson to move promptly in the morning back to Bolton, the nearest point where Johnston could reach the road. Bolton is about twenty miles west of Jackson. I also informed McClernand of the capture of Jackson and sent him the following order: "It is evidently the design of the enemy to get north of us and cross the Big Black, and beat us into Vicksburg. We must not allow them to do this. Turn all your forces towards Bolton station, and make all dispatch in getting there. Move troops by the most direct road from wherever they may be on the receipt of this order." . . .

Johnston stopped on the Canton road only six miles north of Jackson, the night of the 14th. He sent from there to Pemberton dispatches announcing the loss of Jackson, and the following order:

"As soon as the reinforcements are all up, they must be united to the rest of the army. I am anxious to see a force assembled that may be able to inflict a heavy blow upon the enemy. Can Grant supply himself from the Mississippi? Can you not cut him off from it, and above all, should he be compelled to fall back for want of supplies, beat him."

The concentration of my troops was easy, considering the character of the country. McPherson moved along the road parallel with and near the railroad. McClernand's command was, one division ([Alvin] Hovey's) on the road McPherson had to take, but with a start of four miles. One ([Peter] Osterhaus) was at Raymond, on a converging road that intersected the other near Champion's Hill' one ([Eugene] Carr's) had to pass over the same road with Osterhaus, but being back at Mississippi Springs, would not be detained by it; the fourth ([A. J.] Smith's) with [Francis] Blair's division, was near Auburn with a different road to pass over. McClernand faced about and moved promptly. His cavalry from Raymond seized Bolton by half-past nine in the morning, driving out the enemy's pickets and capturing several men.

The night of the 15th Hovey was at Bolton; Carr and Osterhaus were about three miles south, but abreast, facing west; Smith was north of Raymond with Blair in his rear.

McPherson's command, with Logan in front, had marched at seven o'clock, and by four reached Hovey and went into camp; Crocker bivouacked just in Hovey's rear on the Clinton road. Sherman with two divisions, was in Jackson, completing the destruction of roads, bridges and military factories. I rode in person out to Clinton. On my arrival I ordered McClernand to move early in the morning on Edward's station, cautioning him to watch for the enemy and not bring on an engagement unless he felt very certain of success.

I naturally expected that Pemberton would endeavor to obey the orders of his superior, which I have shown were to attack us at Clinton. This, indeed, I knew he could not do; but I felt sure he would make the attempt to reach that point. It turned out, however, that he had decided his superior's plans were impracticable, and consequently determined to move south from Edward's station and get between me and my base. I, however, had no base, having abandoned it more than a week before. On the 15th Pemberton had actually marched south from Edward's station, but the rains had swollen Baker's Creek, which he had to cross, so much that he could not ford it, and the bridges were washed away. This brought him back to the Jackson road, on which there was a good bridge over Baker's Creek.

BELOW: The defensive tactic known as the hollow square is practiced by a Pennsylvania regiment. In the Civil War rising levels of battlefield firepower were making such traditional tactics obsolete, something only a handful of commanders in both armies readily understood.

ABOVE: A Union army battery crosses a stream via a crude ferry. Increasingly during the war, both sides called on their engineer services to devise faster ways to move large formations and heavy matériel over long distances and natural barriers.

RIGHT: Frederick Steele led a division in Sherman's corps during the Vicksburg Campaign. He would later conduct the 1864 Arkansas Campaign.

Some of his troops were marching until midnight to get there. Receiving here early on the 16th a repetition of his order to join Johnston at Clinton, he concluded to obey, and sent a dispatch to his chief, informing him of the route by which he might be expected.

About five o'clock in the morning (16th) two men, who had been employed on the Jackson and Vicksburg railroad, were brought to me. They reported that they had passed through Pemberton's army in the night, and that it was still marching east. They reported him to have eighty regiments of infantry and ten batteries; in all, about twenty-five thousand men.

I had expected to leave Sherman at Jackson another day in order to complete his work; but getting the above information I sent him orders to move with all dispatch to Bolton, and to put one division with an ammunition train on the road at once, with directions to its commander to march with all possible speed until he came up to our rear. Within an hour after receiving this order [Frederick] Steele's division was on the road. At the same time I dispatched to Blair, who was near Auburn, to move with all speed to Edward's station. McClernand was directed to embrace Blair in his command for the present. Blair's division was a part of the 15th army corps (Sherman's); but as it was on its way to join its corps, it naturally struck our left first, now that we had faced about and were moving west. The 15th corps, when it got up, would be on our extreme right. McPherson was directed to get his trains out of the way of the troops, and to follow Hovey's division as closely as possible. McClernand had two roads about three miles apart, converging at Edward's station, over which to march his troops. Hovey's division of his corps had the advance on a third road (the Clinton) still farther north. McClernand was directed to move Blair's and A. J. Smith's divisions by the southernmost of these roads, and Osterhaus and Carr by the middle road. Orders were to move cautiously. . . .

Smith's division on the most southern road was the first to encounter the enemy's pickets, who were speedily driven in. Osterhaus, on the middle road, hearing the firing, pushed his skirmishers forward, found the enemy's pickets and forced them back to the main line. About the same time Hovey encountered the enemy on the northern or direct wagon road from Jackson to Vicksburg. McPherson was hastening up to join Hovey, but was embarrassed by Hovey's trains occupying the road. I was still back at Clinton. McPherson sent me word of the situation, and expressed the wish that I was up. By half-past seven I was on the road and proceeded rapidly to the front, ordering all trains that were in front of troops off the road. When I arrived Hovey's skirmishing amounted almost to a battle.

McClernand was in person on the middle road and had a shorter distance to march to reach the enemy's position than McPherson. I sent him word by a staff officer to push forward and attack. These orders were repeated several times without apparently expediting McClernand's advance.

Champion's Hill, where Pemberton had chosen his position to receive us, whether taken by accident or design, was well selected. It is one of the highest points in that section, and commanded all the ground in range. On the east side of the ridge, which is quite precipitous, is a ravine running first

ABOVE: Union General Edward Otho Cresap Ord and family. Ord, who had fought beside Grant at Corinth, commanded a corps in the final stages of the Vicksburg Campaign.

LEFT: Thomas E.G. Ransom led a brigade in McPherson's corps during the campaign. Grant later called him "the best man I ever had to send on expeditions."

north, then westerly, terminating at Baker's Creek. It was grown up thickly with large trees and undergrowth, making it difficult to penetrate with troops, even when not defended. The ridge occupied by the enemy terminated abruptly where the ravine turns westerly. The left of the enemy occupied the north end of this ridge. The Bolton and Edward's station wagon-road turns almost due south at this point and ascends the ridge, which it follows for about a mile; then turning west, descends by a gentle declivity to Baker's Creek, nearly a mile away. On the west side the slope of the ridge is gradual and is cultivated from near the summit to the creek. There was, when we were there, a narrow belt of timber near the summit west of the road.

From Raymond there is a direct road to Edward's station some three miles west of Champion's Hill. There is one also to Bolton. From this latter road there is still another, leaving it about three and a half miles before reaching Bolton and leads directly to the same station. It was among these two roads that three divisions of McClernand's corps, and Blair of Sherman's, temporarily under McClernand, were moving. Hovey of McClernand's command was with McPherson, farther north on the road from Bolton direct to Edward's station. The middle road comes into the northern road at the point where the latter turns to the west and descends to Baker's Creek; the southern road is still several miles south and does not intersect the others until it reaches Edward's station. Pemberton's lines covered all these

roads, and faced east. Hovey's line, when it first drove in the enemy's pickets, was formed parallel to that of the enemy and confronted his left.

By eleven o'clock the skirmishing had grown into a hard-contested battle. Hovey alone, before other troops could be got to assist him, had captured a battery of the enemy. But he was not able to hold his position and had to abandon the artillery. McPherson brought up his troops as fast as possible, Logan in front, and posted them on the right of Hovey and across the flank of the enemy. Logan reinforced Hovey with one brigade from his division; with his other two he moved farther west to make room for Crocker, who was coming up as rapidly as the roads would admit. Hovey was still being heavily pressed, and was calling on me for more reinforcements. I ordered Crocker, who was now coming up, to send one brigade from his division. McPherson ordered two batteries to be stationed where they nearly enfiladed the enemy's line, and they did good execution.

From Logan's position now a direct forward movement carried him over open fields, in rear of the enemy and in a line parallel with them. He did make exactly this move, attacking, however, the enemy through the belt of woods covering the west slope of the hill for a short distance. Up to this time I had kept my position near Hovey where we were the most heavily pressed; but about noon I moved with a part of my staff by our right around, until I came up with Logan himself. I found him near the road leading

RIGHT: The division led by M.M. Crocker (of McPherson's corps) in action at Jackson on May 14, 1863.

FAR LEFT TOP: Confederate General Carter L. Stevenson fought Grant at Vicksburg and would fight him again at Lookout Mountain.

FAR LEFT BOTTOM: Alfred Cumming led one of the Rebel brigades that tried vainly to lift the Vicksburg siege.

LEFT: Robert K. Scott fought under Grant throughout the Vicksburg Campaign. Not yet a general officer at that time, he would attain a permanent major generalcy by 1865.

command by the left flank around to Hovey. This uncovered the rebel line of retreat, which was soon taken advantage of. . . .

During all this time, Hovey, reinforced as he was by a brigade from Logan and another from Crocker, and by Crocker gallantly coming up with two other brigades on his right, had made several assaults, the last one about the time the road was opened to the rear. The enemy fled precipitately. This was between three and four o'clock. I rode forward, or rather back, to where the middle road intersects the north road, and found the skirmishers of Carr's division just coming in. Osterhaus was farther south and soon after came up with skirmishers advanced in like manner. Hovey's division, and McPherson's two divisions with him, had marched and fought from early dawn, and were not in the best condition to follow the retreating foe. I sent orders to Osterhaus to pursue the enemy, and to Carr, whom I saw personally, I explained the situation and directed him to pursue vigorously as far as the Big Black, and to cross it if he could; Osterhaus to follow him. The pursuit was continued until after dark.

The battle of Champion's Hill lasted about four hours, hard fighting, preceded by two or three hours of skirmishing, some of which almost rose to the dignity of battle. Every man of Hovey's division and of McPherson's two divisions was engaged during the battle. No other part of my command was engaged at all, except that as described before. Osterhaus's and A. J. Smith's divisions had encountered the rebel advanced pickets as early as half-past seven. Their positions were admirable for advancing upon the

down to Baker's Creek. He was actually in command of the only road over which the enemy could retreat; Hovey, reinforced by two brigades from McPherson's command, confronted the enemy's left; Crocker, with two brigades, covered their left flank; McClernand two hours before, had been within two miles and a half of the centre with two divisions, and the two divisions, Blair's and A. J. Smith's, were confronting the rebel right; [T.E.G.] Ransom, with a brigade of [John] McArthur's division of the 17th corps (McPherson's), had crossed the river at Grand Gulf a few days before, and was coming up on their right flank. Neither Logan nor I knew that we had cut off the retreat of the enemy. Just at this juncture a messenger came from Hovey, asking for more reinforcements. There were none to spare. I then gave an order to move McPherson's

RIGHT: One of the South's most brilliant cavalry leaders, Nathan Bedford Forrest had first clashed with Grant at Fort Donelson, then again at Shiloh. During the Vicksburg Campaign he vexed Grant by raiding his rear supply lines.

BELOW: After Vickburg's fall men of the 8th Wisconsin pose with the regimental mascot, an eagle named "Old Abe."

enemy's line. McClernand, with two divisions, was within a few miles of the battlefield long before noon, and in easy hearing. I sent him repeated orders by staff officers fully competent to explain to him the situation. These traversed the wood separating us, without escort, and directed him to push forward; but he did not come. It is true, in front of McClernand there was a small force of the enemy and posted in a good position behind a ravine obstructing his advance; but if he had moved to the right by the road my staff officers had followed the enemy must either have fallen back or been cut off. Instead of this he sent orders to Hovey who belonged to his corps, to join on to his right flank. Hovey was bearing the brunt of the battle at the time. To obey the order he would have had to pull out from the front of the enemy and march back as far as McClernand had to advance to get into battle, and substantially over the same ground. Of course I did not permit Hovey to obey the order of his intermediate superior.

We had in this battle about 15,000 men absolutely engaged. This excludes those that did not get up, all of McClernand's command except Hovey. Our loss was 410 killed, 1,844 wounded and 187 missing. Hovey alone lost 1,200 killed, wounded and missing – more than one-third of his division.

Had McClernand come up with reasonable promptness, or had I known the ground as I did afterwards, I cannot see how Pemberton could have escaped with any organized force. As it was he lost over three thousand killed and wounded and about three thousand captured in battle and in pursuit. [William W.] Loring's division, which was the right of Pemberton's line, was cut off from the retreating army and never got back into Vicksburg. Pemberton himself fell back that night to the Big Black River. His troops did not stop before midnight and many of them left before the general retreat commenced, and no doubt a good part of them returned to their homes. . . .

Though Grant pursued the retreating Pemberton closely, the Confederate General narrowly succeeded in getting his troops back inside the formidable Vicksburg defenses before Grant could catch them. On arriving at Vicksburg, Grant almost immediately (May 22) ordered a general assault on the Confederate lines. It was so bloodily re-pulsed that Grant was obliged to settle in for what looked like a long and – Johnston was still somewhere at his back – potentially dangerous siege.

My line was more than fifteen miles long, extending from Haines' Bluff to Vicksburg, thence to Warrenton. The line of the enemy was about seven. In addition to this, having an enemy at Canton and Jackson, in our rear, who was being constantly reinforced, we required a second line of defence facing the other way. I had not troops enough under my command to man these. General Halleck appreciated the situation and, without being asked, forwarded reinforcements with all possible dispatch.

The ground about Vicksburg is admirable for defence. On the north it is about two hundred feet above the Mississippi River at the highest point and very much cut up by the washing rains; the ravines were grown up with cane and underbush, while the sides and tops were covered with a dense forest. Farther south the ground flattens out somewhat, and was in cultivation. But here, too, it was cut up by ravines and small streams. The enemy's line of defence followed the crest of a ridge from the river north of the city eastward, then southerly around to the Jackson road, full three miles back of the city; thence in a southwesterly direction to the river. Deep ravines of the description given

ABOVE: Federal batteries in action during the siege of Vicksburg exchange fire with their better-situated enemy counterparts on the heights.

ABOVE: Union army barracks set up in Vicksburg after the city's surrender.

lay in front of these defences. As there is a succession of gullies, cut out by rains along the side of the ridge, the line was necessarily very irregular. To follow each of these spurs with intrenchments, so as to command the slopes on either side, would have lengthened their line very much. Generally therefore, or in many places, their line would run from near the head of one gully nearly straight to the head of another, and an outer work triangular in shape, generally open in the rear, was thrown up on the point; with a few men in this outer work they commanded the approaches to the main line completely.

The work to be done, to make our position as strong against the enemy as his was against us, was very great. The problem was also complicated by our wanting our line as near that of the enemy as possible. . . .

We had no siege guns except six thirty-two-pounders, and there were none at the West to draw from. Admiral Porter, however, supplied us with a battery of navy-guns of large calibre, and with these, and the field artillery used in the campaign, the siege began. . . .

In no place were our lines more than six hundred yards from the enemy. It was necessary, therefore, to cover our men by something more than the ordinary parapet. To give additional protection sand bags, bullet-proof, were placed along the tops of the parapets far enough apart to make loopholes for musketry. On top of these, logs were put. By these means the men were enabled to walk about erect when off duty, without fear of annoyance from sharpshooters. The enemy used in their defence

RIGHT: At one point (June) in the siege of Vicksburg Union troops tried mining a part of the defending line. They were unable, however, to fight their way through the breach the explosion created. They exploded a second mine on July 1 but this time made no effort to follow up.

explosive musket-balls, no doubt thinking that, bursting over our men in the trenches, they would do some execution; but I do not remember a single case where a man was injured by a piece of one of these shells. When they were hit and the ball exploded, the wound was terrible. In these cases a solid ball would have hit as well. Their use is barbarous, because they produce increased suffering without any corresponding advantage to those using them. . . .

The siege dragged on through the remainder of May and then through June. Slowly the besiegers compressed the defenders' lines, but by July 1 Vicksburg's defenses had still not been breached. Meantime, evidence was growing that Johnston's long-threatened attack from the east would probably be launched sometime in early July, and Grant ordered that a major assault on the city would be made on July 6, hoping thereby to eliminate the danger of having to fight simultaneously on two fronts before Johnston struck. In the event, neither Johnston's nor Grant's attacks materialized, for on July 3, the same day that Robert E. Lee met defeat at Gettysburg, Pemberton opened negotiations for Vicksburg's surrender. Grant offered generous terms, which Pemberton quickly accepted, and the surrender became a fact on July 4, 1863.

I rode into Vicksburg with the troops, and went to the river to exchange congratulations with the navy upon our joint victory. At that time I found that many of the citizens had been living under ground. The ridges upon which Vicksburg is built, and those back in the Big Black, are composed of a deep yellow clay of great tenacity. Where roads and streets are cut through, perpendicular banks are left and stand as well as if composed of stone. The magazines of the enemy were made by running passage-ways into this clay at places where there were deep cuts. Many citizens secured places of safety for their families by carving out rooms in these embankments. A door-way in these cases would be cut in a high bank, starting from the level of the road or street, and after running in a few feet a room of the size required was carved out of the clay, the dirt being removed by the door-way. In some instances I saw where the two rooms were cut

out, for a single family, with a door-way in the clay wall separating them. Some of these were carpeted and furnished with considerable elaboration. In these the occupants were fully secure from the shells of the navy, which were dropped into the city night and day without intermission.

I returned to my old headquarters outside in the afternoon, and did not move into the town until the sixth. On the afternoon of the fourth I sent Captain Wm. M. Dunn of my staff to Cairo, the nearest point where the telegraph could be reached, with a dispatch to the general-in-chief. It was as follows:

"The enemy surrendered this morning. The only terms allowed is their parole as prisoners of war. This I regard as a great advantage to us at this moment. It saves, probably, several days in the capture, and leaves troops and transports ready for immediate service. Sherman, with a large force, moves immediately on Johnston, to drive him from the State. I will send troops to the relief of Banks, and return the 9th army corps to Burnside."

This news, with the victory of Gettysburg won the same day, lifted a great load of anxiety from the minds of the President, his Cabinet and the loyal people all over the North. The fate of the Confederacy was sealed when Vicksburg fell. Much hard fighting was to be done afterwards and many precious lives were to be sacrificed; but the *morale* was with the supporters of the Union ever after. . . .

ABOVE: During the siege many Vicksburg citizens, in order to escape the effects of the Union bombardment, took to living in artificial caves dug into the sides of bluffs. Life in these caves probably was not quite as hard as this sentimental Southern sketch implies. Grant was impressed with how well furnished some such dwellings were when he viewed them after the city's capitulation on July 4, 1863.

Chapter IV

The Battle of Chattanooga

BELOW: Since the beginning of 1863 General William S. Rosecrans, a good tactician, had steadily been forcing the Confederate army of Braxton Bragg back through Tennessee toward Chattanooga. All his hard-won gains were nearly undone, however, when Bragg beat him at the Battle of Chickamauga in September.

Soon after the surrender of Vicksburg, Port Hudson (as expected) fell to Federal troops. The entire Mississippi was now in Union hands. It all amounted to an immense strategic victory, but of course it still had to be exploited. A potentially very promising avenue for such exploitation lay in a campaign that Federal General William S. Rosecrans was conducting against Confederate forces under General Braxton Bragg in central Tennessee. Since early summer Rosecrans had steadily (if somewhat slowly) been driving Bragg southeast towards the vital Confederate rail center of Chattanooga. The

alarmed C.S.A. government in Richmond detached General James Longstreet's corps from Lee's army in Virginia and hurried it by rail to reinforce Bragg, but before Longstreet could arrive, Rosecrans, by adroit maneuvering, had, in early September, forced Bragg to evacuate Chattanooga. When Rosecrans attempted to pursue Bragg, however, he permitted his troops to become strung out in unfavorable terrain, and on September 19-20 Bragg, now reinforced by Longstreet, dealt Rosecrans a shattering blow in the Battle of Chickamauga. Rosecrans retreated to Chattanooga, where Bragg surrounded him and held him in a state of siege.

Now it was Washington's turn to be alarmed, and Lincoln and his advisers turned to Grant to retrieve the situation. Grant was given command of a newly-formed Division of the Mississippi (which included everything from that river to the Appalachians) and was dispatched to Chattanooga. Grant arrived in the city on October 24, relieved Rosecrans, and gave executive control of his army to the able George H. Thomas, now famous as the "Rock of Chickamauga." Within a month Grant had re-opened supply lines into Chattanooga, had strongly reinforced the Federal army in the city, and was ready to resume the offensive. Seeking to forestall Grant, Confederate President Jefferson Davis detached Longstreet and 15,000 troops from Bragg's force to move northeast and attack Union General Ambrose Burnside in Knoxville. As Davis had hoped, this move worried Washington and resulted in considerable pressure on Grant to send reinforcements to Burnside. But Grant resisted all efforts to weaken his army, and in the end it was Bragg's army, not Grant's, that Davis's too-clever maneuver weakened.

ABOVE: Fought on September 19-20, 1863, the Battle of Chickamauga was one of the last clear-cut Confederate victories. A confusion in the execution of his orders opened a hole in Rosecrans's line, which Longstreet, who had just reinforced Bragg, devastatingly exploited. The beaten Federals retreated to Chattanooga, where Bragg's army besieged them.

LEFT: Union General Ambrose Burnside (center) in an 1861 photograph. In the fall of 1863 he was in Knoxville. By attacking him there, Southern strategists hoped to divert Grant from mounting a new offensive from Chattanooga.

Grant began his offensive on November 24, Sherman making some headway against the main enemy force on Missionary Ridge, to the east of the city, and General Joseph Hooker capturing a secondary Rebel position a little to the south on Lookout Mountain. Now Grant was ready to concentrate all his forces for a major assault on Bragg's well-entrenched army on steep-sloped Missionary Ridge.

BELOW: Union General Joseph Hooker, who had been badly beaten at Chancellorsville earlier in 1863, was one of Grant's weaker lieutenants at Chattanooga.

The morning of the 25th opened clear and bright, and the whole field was in full view from the top of Orchard Knob. It remained so all day. Bragg's headquarters were in full view, and officers – presumably staff officers – could be seen coming and going constantly.

The point of ground which Sherman had carried on the 24th was almost disconnected from the main ridge occupied by the enemy. A low pass, over which there is a wagon road crossing the hill, and near

which there is a railroad tunnel, intervenes between the two hills. The problem now was to get to the main ridge. The enemy was fortified on the point; and back farther, where the ground was still higher, was a second fortification commanding the first. Sherman was out as soon as it was light enough to see, and by sunrise his command was in motion. Three brigades held the hill already gained. Morgan L. Smith moved along the east base of Missionary Ridge; [G.] Loomis along the west base, supported by two brigades of John E. Smith's division; and [J.M.] Corse with his brigade was between the two, moving directly towards the hill to be captured. The ridge is steep and heavily wooded on the east side, where M. L. Smith's troops were advancing, but cleared and with a more gentle slope on the west side. The troops advanced rapidly and carried the extreme end of the rebel works. Morgan L. Smith advanced to a point which cut the enemy off from the railroad bridge and the means of bringing up supplies by rail from Chickamauga Station, where the main depot was located. The enemy made brave and strenuous efforts to drive our troops from the position we had gained, but without suc-

cess. The contest lasted for two hours. Corse, a brave and efficient commander, was badly wounded in this assault. Sherman now threatened both Bragg's flanks and his stores, and made it necessary for him to weaken other points of his line to strengthen his right. From the position I occupied I could see column after column of Bragg's forces moving against Sherman. Every Confederate gun that could be brought to bear upon the Union forces was concentrated upon him. . . . This was what I wanted. But it had now got to be late in the afternoon, and I had expected before this to see Hooker crossing the ridge in the neighborhood of Rossville and compelling Bragg to mass in that direction also.

The enemy had evacuated Lookout Mountain during the night, as I expected he would. In crossing the valley he burned the bridge over Chattanooga Creek, and did all he could to obstruct the roads behind him. Hooker was off bright and early, with no obstructions in his front but distance and the destruction above named. He was detained four hours crossing Chattanooga Creek, and thus was lost the immediate advantage I expected from his forces. His reaching Bragg's

ABOVE: Lookout Mountain, as viewed from the Tennessee. It was Hooker's assignment to take the mountain on November 24. He did so but was then dilatory in repositioning his troops to join in the main attack on Missionary Ridge the next day.

RIGHT: A view of Chattanooga looking southwest toward Lookout Mountain.

OPPOSITE: The Union charge up Missionary Ridge.

OPPOSITE BOTTOM: The landing from which the Union forces in Chattanooga received most of their supplies.

BELOW: A Union map of the Chattanooga battle area.

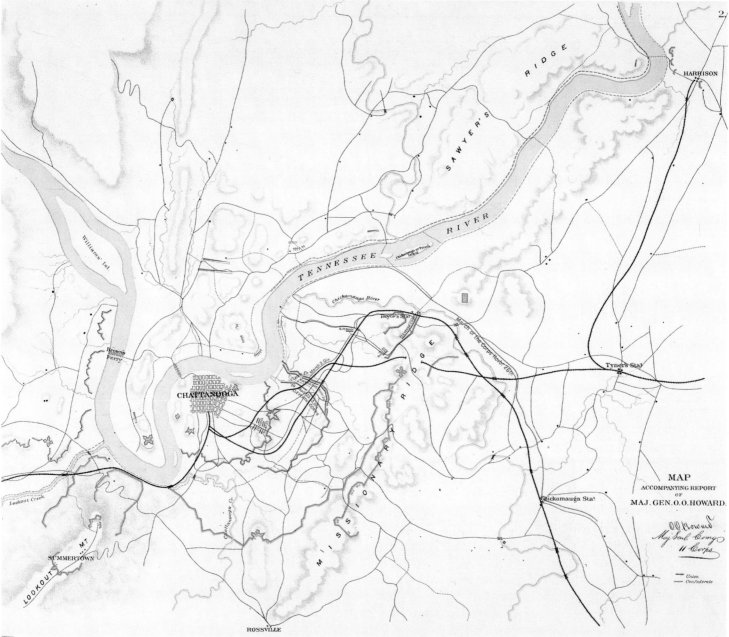

ABOVE: A photograph taken after the battle shows well the terrain the Union army had to cross in attacking Missionary Ridge.

RIGHT: Among the Confederate victors at Chickamauga was Montgomery Dent Corse, who led the brigade that George Pickett had once commanded.

OPPOSITE TOP: After Rebel forces were expelled from the Chattanooga area Union engineers built this bridge over the Tennessee.

flank and extending across it was to be the signal for Thomas's assault of the ridge. But Sherman's condition was getting so critical that the assault for his relief could not be delayed any longer.

[Philip] Sheridan's and [Thomas] Wood's divisions had been lying under arms from early morning, ready to move the instant the signal was given. I now directed Thomas to order the charge at once. a . . [I]n an incredibly short time loud cheering was heard, and [Wood] and Sheridan were driving the enemy's advance before them towards Missionary Ridge. The Confederates were strongly intrenched on the crest of the ridge in front of us, and had a second line half-way down and another at the base. Our men drove the troops in front of the lower line of rifle-pits so rapidly, and followed them so closely, that rebel and Union troops went over the first line of works almost at the same time. Many rebels were captured and sent to the rear under the fire of their own friends higher up the hill. Those that were not captured retreated, and were pursued. The retreating hordes being between friends and pursuers caused the enemy to fire high to avoid killing their own men. In fact, on

that occasion the Union soldier nearest the enemy was in the safest position. Without awaiting further orders or stopping to re-form, on our troops went to the second line of works; over that and on for the crest – thus effectually carrying out my orders of the 18th for the battle and of the 24th for his charge.

I watched their progress with intense interest. The fire along the rebel line was terrific. Cannon and musket balls filled the air: but the damage done was in small proportion to the ammunition expended. The pursuit continued until the crest was reached, and soon our men were seen climbing over the Confederate barriers at different points in front of both Sheridan's and Wood's divisions. The retreat of the enemy along most of his line was precipitate and the panic so great that Bragg and his officers lost all control over their men. Many were captured, and thousands threw away their arms in their flight. . . .

The victory at Chattanooga was won against great odds, considering the advantage the enemy had of position, and was accomplished more easily than was expected by reason of Bragg's making several grave mistakes: first, in sending away his

ablest corps commander with over twenty thousand troops; second, in sending away a division of troops on the eve of battle; third, in placing so much of a force on the plain in front of his impregnable position.

It was known that Mr. Jefferson Davis had visited Bragg on Missionary Ridge a short time before my reaching Chattanooga. It was reported and believed that he had come out to reconcile a serious difference be-

ABOVE: The small frame house in Chattanooga where Sherman made his headquarters during the siege of the city.

RIGHT: Grant (left) surveys
the scene of Joseph Hooker's
victory on Lookout Mountain.

BELOW: The troops of General
George Thomas begin their
charge at Missionary Ridge.

tween Bragg and Longstreet, and finding this difficult to do, planned the campaign against Knoxville, to be conducted by the latter general. I had known both Bragg and Longstreet before the war, the latter very well. We had been three years at West Point together, and, after my graduation, for a time in the same regiment. Then we served together in the Mexican War. I had known Bragg in Mexico, and met him occasionally subsequently. I could well understand how there might be an irreconcilable difference between them.

Bragg was a remarkably intelligent and well-informed man, professionally and otherwise. He was also thoroughly upright. But he was possessed of an irascible temper, and was naturally disputatious. A man of the highest moral character and the most correct habits, yet in the old army he was in frequent trouble. As a subordinate he was always on the lookout to catch his commanding officer infringing his prerogatives; as a post commander he was equally vigilant to detect the slightest neglect, even of the most trivial order. . . .

Longstreet was an entirely different man. He was brave, honest, intelligent, a very capable soldier, subordinate to his superiors, just and kind to his subordinates, but jealous of his own rights, which he had the courage to maintain. He was never on the lookout to detect a slight, but saw one as soon as anybody when intentionally given.

It may be that Longstreet was not sent to Knoxville for the reason stated, but because Mr. Davis had an exalted opinion of his own military genius, and thought he saw a chance of "killing two birds with one stone." On several occasions during the war he came to the relief of the Union army by means of his *superior military genius*. . . .

BELOW: The Battle of Lookout Mountain, as portrayed by the print-makers Kurz and Allison.

Chapter V

The Advance on Richmond

Grant's triumph at Chattanooga hurled Bragg's disorganized forces back into Georgia and made it possible for Grant to send massive reinforcements (two full corps under Sherman) to Burnside, thus dispelling the threat to Knoxville. Though some mopping up remained to be done, the Union was now effectively in control of Tennessee and poised to deliver, when the spring campaigning season began, the long-awaited thrust from the west to east that would cut the Old South in half.

Grant had assumed that this was to be his next assignment, but Washington had other plans for him. In March 1864 he was summoned to Washington, made a lieutenant-general (the highest rank the government had the power to confer), and placed in supreme command of all the armies of the Union. Now he was responsible not only for planning the eastward thrust out of Tennessee but all actions taken by Union armies everywhere.

Grant soon concluded that Union strategy for 1864 should consist of two coordinated major offensives directed at the two biggest Confederate armies then in the field: Robert E. Lee's Army of Northern Virginia and the Army of Tennessee (Bragg's old command, now under the formidable Joseph E. Johnston), currently in the vicinity of Dalton, Georgia. A third, smaller, and essentially diversionary offensive under Nathaniel Banks was to be launched from New Orleans against Mobile and Montgomery. (In the event, it failed.) Grant somewhat reluctantly

BELOW: When he was planning Union army operations for 1864, newly-created Lieutenant General Grant worked in this headquarters on 17th Street in Washington, D.C.

ABOVE: Fort Stevens, part of the outer defense perimeter of Washington, D.C., would bear the brunt of Early's diversionary attack on the city in July 1864.

LEFT: Grant with his eight-man personal staff in the field in 1864.

RIGHT: A curious European print of (l. to r.) Sheridan, Sherman, and Grant, wherein not one of the three is the least bit recognizable.

OPPOSITE TOP: Simultaneous with Grant's 1864 advance on Richmond was Sherman's march towards Atlanta. Shown here is one of the few mistakes Sherman made in the campaign: a frontal attack on strong defenses at Kenesaw Mountain.

OPPOSITE: Downtown Atlanta in 1864. News of Sherman's capture of the city was a political godsend to Lincoln and may have saved him from defeat in the 1864 election.

decided that the Georgia offensive, aimed at Atlanta and Savannah, could safely be left to his favorite lieutenant, William Tecumseh Sherman, and that he, Grant, would be needed to supervise the more dangerous effort by George Meade's Army of the Potomac to get past Lee and capture the Confederate capital of Richmond, Virginia.

Both big offensives began on May 4. Sherman, in a hard-fought war of maneuver, slowly forced Johnston back, but it was not until after Jefferson Davis had replaced Johnston with the less competent John B. Hood that Sherman was able to reach Atlanta and not until September 1 that the Georgia capital finally fell. It was nevertheless a very important victory, especially because 1864 was a presidential election year. As Grant put it: "The news of Sherman's success . . . set the country all aglow. . . . It was followed later by [Philip] Sheridan's campaign in the Shenandoah Valley; and these two campaigns probably had more effect in settling the election of the following November than all the speeches, all the bonfires, and all the parading with banners and bands of music in the North."

The two military successes may finally have guaranteed Lincoln's reelection, but they came precariously *late in a year that had brought Washington all-too-little cheering news from the battlefronts, and especially from the Eastern battlefront. Grant had never before faced an opponent of Lee's caliber, and from their very first encounter he must have realized that he was in for a long, difficult, and bloody campaign.*

Soon after midnight, May 3rd-4th, the Army of the Potomac moved out from its position north of the Rapidan, to start upon that memorable campaign, destined to result in the capture of the Confederate capital and the army defending it. This was not to be accomplished, however, without as desperate fighting as the world has ever witnessed; not to be consummated in a day, a week, a month, or a single season. The losses inflicted, and endured, were destined to be severe; but the armies now confronting each other had already been in deadly conflict for a period of three years, with immense losses in killed, by death from sickness, captured and wounded; and neither had made any real progress toward accomplishing the final end. It is true the Confederates had, so far, held their capital, and they claimed this to be their sole object. But previously they had boldly proclaimed their intention to capture Philadelphia, New York, and the National Capital, and had

made several attempts to do so, and once or twice had come fearfully near making their boast good – too near for complacent contemplation by the loyal North. They had also come near losing their own capital on at least one occasion. So here was a stand-off. The campaign now begun was destined to result in heavier losses, to both armies, in a given time, than any previously suffered; but the carnage was to be limited to a single year, and to accomplish all that had been anticipated or desired at the beginning in that time. We had to have hard fighting to achieve this. . . .

The Army of the Potomac was composed of three infantry and one cavalry corps, commanded respectively by Generals W. S. Hancock, G. K. Warren, John Sedgwick and P. H. Sheridan. The artillery was commanded by General Henry J. Hunt. . . .

The 5th corps, General Warren commanding, was in advance on the right, and marched directly for Germania Ford, preceded by one division of cavalry, under General J. H. Wilson. General Sedgwick followed Warren with the 6th corps. Germania Ford was nine or ten miles below the right of Lee's line. Hancock, with the 2d corps, moved by another road, farther east, directly upon Ely's Ford, six miles below Germania, preceded by [D. M.] Gregg's division of cavalry, and followed by the artillery. [A. T. A.] Torbert's division of cavalry was left north of the Rapidan, for the time, to picket the river and prevent the enemy from crossing and getting into our rear. The cavalry seized the two crossings before daylight, drove the enemy's pickets guarding them away, and by six o'clock A.M. had the pontoons laid ready for the crossing of the infantry and artillery. This was undoubtedly a surprise to Lee. The fact that the movement was unopposed proves this.

[General Ambrose] Burnside, with the 9th corps, was left back at Warrenton, guarding the railroad from Bull Run forward to preserve control of it in case our crossing the Rapidan should be long delayed. He was instructed, however, to advance at once on receiving notice that the army had crossed; and a dispatch was sent to him a little after one P.M. giving the information that our crossing had been successful. . . .

As soon as the crossing of the infantry was assured, the cavalry pushed forward, Wilson's division by Wilderness Tavern to Parker's store, on the Orange Plank Road; Gregg to the left towards Chancellorsville. Warren followed Wilson and reached the Wilderness Tavern by noon, took position there and intrenched. Sedgwick followed Warren. He was across the river and in camp on the south bank, on the right of Warren, by sundown. Hancock, with the 2d corps, moved parallel with Warren and camped about six miles east of him. Before night all the troops, and by the evening of the 5th the trains of more than four thousand wagons, were safely on the south side of the river. . . .

On discovering the advance of the Army of the Potomac, Lee ordered [A. P.] Hill, [Richard] Ewell and [James] Longstreet, each commanding corps, to move to the right to attack us, Hill on the Orange Plank Road, Longstreet to follow on the same road. Longstreet was at this time – middle of the afternoon – at Gordonsville, twenty or more miles away. Ewell was ordered by the

OPPOSITE TOP: James Wilson (sprawling on the steps) led a division in Sheridan's cavalry corps when Grant's 1864 campaign started. He would command his own corps before the year's end.

OPPOSITE: Another divisional commander in Sheridan's corps was David McM. Gregg (seated, right), a veteran of Gettysburg.

Orange Pike. He was near by and arrived some four miles east of Mine Run before bivouacking for the night.

My orders were given through General Meade for an early advance on the morning of the 5th. Warren was to move to Parker's store, and Wilson's cavalry – then at Parker's store – to move on to Craig's meeting-house. Sedgwick followed Warren, closing in on his right. The Army of the Potomac was facing to the west, though our advance was made to the south, except when facing the enemy. Hancock was to move south-westward to join on the left of Warren, his left to reach to Shady Grove Church.

At six o'clock before reaching Parker's store, Warren discovered the enemy. He sent word back to this effect, and was ordered to halt and prepare to meet and attack him. [H. G.] Wright, with his division of Sedgwick's corps, was ordered, by any road he could find to join on to Warren's right, and [George] Getty with his division, also of Sedgwick's corps, was ordered to move rapidly by Warren's rear and get on his left. . . .

It was my plan then, as it was on all other occasions, to take the initiative whenever the enemy could be drawn from his intrenchments if we were not intrenched ourselves. . . . Warren was, therefore, ordered to attack as soon as he could prepare for it. At nine o'clock Hancock was ordered to come up to the support of Getty. He himself arrived

RIGHT: Union General George Washington Getty, a division commander in John Sedgwick's corps, was in the thick of the fighting in the Battle of the Wilderness, where he was severely wounded.

between 4 and 5 PM 9th May 64

Rebel advance through the smoke and seizure of a part of the breast work in Brock road. The logs had caught fire — ARW.

at Getty's front about noon, but his troops were yet far in the rear. Getty was directed to hold his position at all hazards until relieved. About this hour Warren was ready, and attacked with favorable though not decisive results. ... At two o'clock Hancock's troops began to arrive, and immediately he was ordered to join Getty and attack the enemy. ...

Fighting between Hancock and Hill continued until night put a close to it. Neither side made any special progress.

After the close of the battle on the 5th of May my orders were given for the following morning. We knew Longstreet with 12,000 men was on his way to join Hill's right, near the Brock Road, and might arrive during the night. I was anxious that the rebels should not take the initiative in the morning, and therefore ordered Hancock to make an assault at 4:30 o'clock. Meade asked to have the hour changed to six. Deferring to his wishes as far as I was willing, the order was modified and five was fixed as the hour to move.

Hancock had now fully one-half of the Army of the Potomac. [James] Wadsworth with his division, which had arrived the night before, lay in a line perpendicular to that

held by Hill, and to the right of Hancock. He was directed to move at the same time, and to attack Hill's left.

Burnside, who was coming up with two divisions, was directed to get in between Warren and Wadsworth, and attack as soon as he could get in position to do so. Sedgwick and Warren were to make attacks in their front, to detain as many of the enemy as they could and to take advantage of any attempt to reinforce Hill from that quarter. Burnside was ordered if he should succeed in breaking the enemy's centre, to swing around to the left and envelop the right of Lee's army. ...

Hancock was ready to advance by the hour named, but learning in time that Longstreet was moving a part of his corps by the Catharpin Road, thus threatening his left flank, sent a division of infantry, commanded by General [Francis] Barlow, with all his artillery, to cover the approaches by which Longstreet was expected. This disposition was made in time to attack as ordered. Hancock moved by the left of the Orange Plank Road, and Wadsworth by the right of it. The fighting was desperate for about an hour, when the army began to break up in great confusion.

ABOVE: An on-the-scene sketch by battlefield artist Alfred R. Waud depicts some of the fighting on the second day of the Battle of the Wilderness. (Note: the date at the top of the sketch should read "6th May," not "9th May".)

103

ABOVE: A battlefield sketch by artist Edwin Forbes shows Union troops on the Brock Road on May 11. Five days earlier this had been the scene of intensely bloody fighting in the Battle of the Wilderness.

RIGHT: Harvard-man Francis Barlow, who led a division in Winfield Scott Hancock's II Corps, fought fiercely to stem the tide of Longstreet's advance on May 6. After the war Barlow, as New York's attorney general, prosecuted Tamany Hall's famous William "Boss" Tweed.

I believed then, and see no reason to change that opinion now, that if the country had been such that Hancock and his command could have seen the confusion and panic in the lines of the enemy, it would have been taken advantage of so effectually that Lee would not have made another stand outside of his Richmond defences. . . .

Hancock followed Hill's retreating forces, in the morning, a mile or more. He maintained this position until, along in the afternoon, Longstreet came upon him. The retreating column of Hill meeting reinforcements that had not yet been engaged, became encouraged and returned with them. They were enabled, from the density of the forest, to approach within a few hundred yards of our advance before being discovered. Falling upon a brigade of Hancock's corps thrown to the advance, they swept it away almost instantly. The enemy followed up his advantage and soon came upon [Gershom] Mott's division, which fell back in great confusion. Hancock made dispositions to hold his advanced position, but after holding it for a time, fell back into the position that he had held in the morning, which was strongly intrenched. In this engagement the intrepid Wadsworth while trying to rally his men was mortally

BELOW: Union General Horatio Gouverneur Wright led VI Corps from the Wilderness through to Appomattox.

ABOVE: The great Robert E. Lee, on his horse Traveller.

OPPOSITE TOP: Union cavalry General George A. Custer (right foreground) in 1861, when he was a lieutenant.

OPPOSITE: An Alfred R. Waud sketch of Grant writing out a telegraph message during the 1864 campaign.

wounded and fell into the hands of the enemy. The enemy followed up, but made no immediate attack.

The Confederate General [Micah] Jenkins was killed and Longstreet seriously wounded in this engagement. Longstreet had to leave the field, not to resume command for many weeks. His loss was a severe one to Lee, and compensated in a great measure for the mishap, or misapprehensions, which had fallen to our lot during the day. . . .

At 4:15 in the afternoon Lee attacked our left. His line moved up to within a hundred yards of ours and opened a heavy fire. This status was maintained for about half an hour. Then a part of Mott's division and [J. H. H.] Ward's brigade of [David] Birney's division gave way and retired in disorder. The enemy under R. H. Anderson took advan-

tage of this and pushed through our line, planting their flags on a part of the intrenchments not on fire. But owing to the efforts of Hancock, their success was but temporary. [Samuel] Carroll, of [John] Gibbon's division, moved at a double quick with his brigade and drove back the enemy, inflicting great loss. Fighting had continued from five in the morning sometimes along the whole line, at other times only in places. The ground fought over had varied in width, but averaged three-quarters of a mile. The killed, and many of the severely wounded, of both armies, lay within this belt where it was impossible to reach them. The woods were set on fire by the bursting shells, and the conflagration raged. The wounded who had not strength to move themselves were either suffocated or burned to death. Finally the fire communicated with our breastworks, in

places. Being constructed of wood, they burned with great fury. But the battle still raged, our men firing through the flames until it became too hot to remain longer. . . .

During the night all of Lee's army withdrew within their intrenchments. On the morning of the 7th General [George A.] Custer drove the enemy's cavalry from Catharpin Furnace to Todd's Tavern. Pickets and skirmishers were sent along our entire front to find the position of the enemy. Some went as far as a mile and a half before finding him. But Lee showed no disposition to come out of his works. There was no battle during the day, and but little firing except in Warren's front; he being directed about noon to make reconnoissance in force. This drew some sharp firing, but there was no attempt on the part of Lee to drive him back. This ended the Battle of the Wilderness. . . .

ABOVE: An artist's somewhat romantic version of Grant leading his troops in the fruitless and costly Battle of Spottsylvania Court House, which took place soon after the Battle of the Wilderness.

More desperate fighting has not been witnessed on this continent than that of the 5th and 6th of May. Our victory consisted in having successfully crossed a formidable stream, almost in the face of an enemy, and in getting the army together as a unit. We gained an advantage on the morning of the 6th, which, if it had been followed up, must have proven very decisive. In the evening the enemy gained an advantage; but was speedily repulsed. As we stood at the close, the two armies were relatively in about the same condition to meet each other as when the river divided them. But the fact of having safely crossed was a victory.

Our losses in the Wilderness were very severe. Those of the Confederates must have been even more so; but I have no means of speaking with accuracy upon this point. The Germania Ford bridge was transferred to Ely's Ford to facilitate the transportation of the wounded to Washington. . . .

The Battle of the Wilderness set the pattern for the nightmarish campaign that was to follow. In two days of inconclusive fighting the North had lost 2,246 killed and 12,073 wounded, but Grant was determined not to let up the pressure on the enemy and quickly ordered a flanking movement around Lee's right wing to bring the Union army to Spottsylvania Court House. Lee anticipated the tactic, moved his forces accordingly, and was entrenched in Spottsylvania when Grant arrived. Grant attacked on May 12, made only token headway, and suffered 6800 more casualties. Again Grant wheeled his army to the left around Lee's flank, and again Lee countermaneuvered so as to block Grant's advance on the North Anna River. There followed another stalemated battle, another Union slide to the left, and now the two armies faced one another again at Cold Harbor.

The night of [May] 30th Lee's position was substantially from Atlee's Station on the Virginia Central Railroad south and east to the vicinity of Cold Harbor. Ours was: The left of Warren's corps was on the Shady Grove Road, extending to the Mechanicsville Road and about three miles south of the Totopoto-

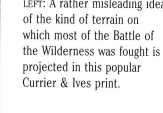

LEFT: A rather misleading idea of the kind of terrain on which most of the Battle of the Wilderness was fought is projected in this popular Currier & Ives print.

BELOW: A U.S. Army map shows the general positions of the two armies in the Battle of the Wilderness and gives as well a good impression of how densely wooded the area was.

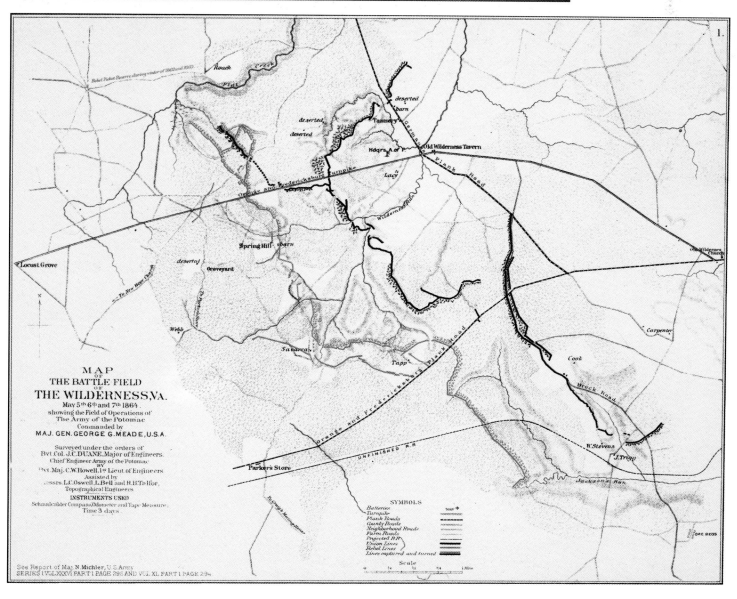

MAP
OF
THE BATTLE FIELD
OF
THE WILDERNESS, VA.
May 5th 6th and 7th 1864.
showing the Field of Operations of
The Army of the Potomac
Commanded by
MAJ. GEN. GEORGE G. MEADE, U.S.A.

Surveyed under the orders of
Bvt Col. J.C. DUANE, Major of Engineers,
Chief Engineer Army of the Potomac
BY
Bvt. Maj. C.W. Howell, 1st Lieut of Engineers
Assisted by
Messrs. L.C. Oswell, L. Bell and R.B. Talfor,
Topographical Engineers

INSTRUMENTS USED
Schmalcalder Compass, Odometer and Tape Measure.
Time 3 days.

RIGHT: By 1864 railroads had become crucial instruments of war, not only for the rapid movement of men and supplies but also as platforms for mobile artillery. This big 32-lb Confederate rail gun, complete with a protective mantlet, is typical of the new forms of artillery that appeared during the last two years of the Civil War. This particular gun was used at Petersburg and perhaps even earlier in the 1864 campaign.

moy. Burnside to his right, then Hancock, and [H. G.] Wright on the extreme right, extending towards Hanover Court House, six miles south-east of it. Sheridan with two divisions of cavalry was watching our left front towards Cold Harbor. Wilson with his division on our right was sent to get on the Virginia Central Railroad and destroy it as far back as possible. He got possession of Hanover Court House the next day after a skirmish with [P. M. B.] Young's cavalry brigade. The enemy attacked Sheridan's pickets, but reinforcements were sent up and the attack was speedily repulsed and the enemy followed some distance towards Cold Harbor. . . .

On the 31st Sheridan advanced to near Old Cold Harbor. He found it intrenched and occupied by cavalry and infantry. A hard fight ensued but the place was carried. The enemy well knew the importance of Cold Harbor to us, and seemed determined that we should not hold it. He returned with such a large force that Sheridan was about withdrawing without making any effort to hold it against such odds; but about the time he commenced the evacuation he received orders to hold the place at all hazards, until reinforcements could be sent to him. He speedily turned the rebel works to face against them and placed his men in position for defence. Night came on before the enemy was ready for assault.

Wright's corps was ordered early in the evening to march directly to Cold Harbor passing by the rear of the army. It was expected to arrive by daylight or before; but the night was dark and the distance great, so that it was nine o'clock the 1st of June before it reached its destination. Before the arrival of Wright the enemy had made two assaults on Sheridan, both of which were repulsed with heavy loss to the enemy. Wright's corps coming up, there was no further assault on Cold Harbor.

[Corps Commander General William F.] Smith, who was coming up from White House, was also directed to march directly to Cold Harbor, and was expected early on the morning of the 1st of June; but by some blunder the order which reached Smith directed him to Newcastle instead of Cold Harbor. Through this blunder Smith did not reach his destination until three o'clock in the afternoon, and then with tired and worn-out men from their long and dusty march. He landed twelve thousand five hundred men from [Benjamin] Butler's command,

BELOW: At a conference held outside Bethesda Church on June 2 Grant leans over the shoulder of General George Meade to consult his map. The disastrous climax of the Battle of Cold Harbor would take place on the following day.

OPPOSITE TOP: The Battle of Cold Harbor according to Kurz & Allison. Grant regretted for the rest of his life the charge he ordered on June 3 against Lee's well-fortified position, for the charge proved to be an extremely costly failure.

OPPOSITE BOTTOM: Grant made up for his mistake at Cold Harbor in his next maneuver, a brilliant end-run that put him well to the south of Lee. The lower picture shows Grant's men crossing the Pamunkey River en route to the James.

but a division was left at White House temporarily and many men had fallen out of ranks in their long march.

Before the removal of Wright's corps from our right, after dark on the 31st, the two lines, Federal and Confederate, were so close together at that point that either side could detect directly any movement made by the other. Finding at daylight that Wright had left his front, Lee evidently divined that he had gone to our left. At all events, soon after light on the 1st of June [R. H.] Anderson, who commanded the corps on Lee's left, was seen moving along Warren's front. Warren was ordered to attack him vigorously in

GRANT'S GREAT CAMPAIGN—GENERAL BARLOW IN FRONT OF THE REBEL WORKS, TWELVE MILES FROM RICHMOND.—FROM A SKETCH BY A. R. WAUD.—[SEE PAGE 116.]

flank, while Wright was directed to move out and get on his front. Warren fired his artillery at the enemy; but lost so much time in making ready that the enemy got by, and at three o'clock he reported the enemy was strongly intrenched in his front, and besides his lines were so long that he had no mass of troops to move with. He seemed to have forgotten that lines in rear of an army hold themselves while their defenders are fighting in their front. Wright reconnoitered some distance to his front: but the enemy finding Old Cold Harbor already taken had halted and fortified some distance west.

By six o'clock in the afternoon Wright and Smith were ready to make an assault. In front of both the ground was clear for several hundred yards, and then became wooded. Both charged across this open space and into the wood, capturing and holding the first line of rifle-pits of the enemy, and also capturing seven or eight hundred prisoners.

While this was going on, the enemy charged Warren three separate times with vigor, but were repulsed each time with loss. There was no officer more capable, nor one more prompt in acting, than Warren when the enemy forced him to it. There was also an attack upon Hancock's and Burnside's corps at the same time; but it was feeble and probably only intended to relieve Anderson who was being pressed by Wright and Smith.

During the night the enemy made frequent attacks with the view of dispossessing us of the important position we had gained, but without effecting their object.

Hancock was moved from his place in line during the night and ordered to the left of Wright. I expected to take the offensive on the morning of the 2d, but the night was so

BELOW: At his headquarters at City Point, on the James, Grant is visited by his wife and youngest son.

dark, the heat and dust so excessive and the roads so intricate and hard to keep, that the head of column only reached Old Cold Harbor at six o'clock, but was in position at 7:30 A.M. Preparations were made for an attack in the afternoon, but did not take place until the next morning. Warren's corps was moved to the left to connect with Smith: Hancock's corps was got into position to the left of Wright's, and Burnside was moved to Bethesda Church in reserve. While Warren and Burnside were making these changes the enemy came out several times and attacked them, capturing several hundred prisoners. The attacks were repulsed, but not followed up as they should have been. I was so annoyed at this that I directed Meade to instruct his corps commanders that they should seize all such opportunities when they occurred, and not wait for orders, all of our manoeuvres being made for the very purpose of getting the enemy out of his cover.

On this day [J. H.] Wilson returned from his raid upon the Virginia Central Railroad, having damaged it considerably. But, like ourselves, the rebels had become experts in repairing such damage. Sherman, in his memoirs, relates an anecdote of his campaign to Atlanta that well illustrates this point. The rebel cavalry lurking in his rear to burn bridges and obstruct his communications had become so disgusted at hearing trains go whistling by within a few hours after a bridge had been burned, that they proposed to try blowing up some of the tunnels. One of them said, "No use, boys, Old Sherman carries duplicate tunnels with him, and will replace them as fast as you can blow them up; better save your powder."

BELOW: An almost certainly forged picture purporting to be of Grant at City Point.

ABOVE: City Point, on the south bank of the James, was to be Grant's headquarters for the remainder of the war. With its access to rail and river traffic, City Point became the main supply base of the Army of the Potomac.

Sheridan was engaged reconnoitering the banks of the Chickahominy, to find crossings and the condition of the roads. He reported favorably.

During the night Lee moved his left up to make his line correspond to ours. His lines extended now from the Totopotomoy to New Cold Harbor. Mine from Bethesda Church by Old Cold Harbor to the Chickahominy, with a division of cavalry guarding our right. An assault was ordered for the 3d, to be made mainly by the corps of Hancock, Wright and Smith; but Warren and Burnside were to support it by threatening Lee's left, and to attack with great earnestness if he should either reinforce more threatened points by drawing from that quarter or if a favorable opportunity should present itself.

The corps commanders were to select the points in their respective fronts where they would make their assaults. The move was to commence at half-past four in the morning. Hancock sent [Francis] Barlow and [John] Gibbon forward at the appointed hour, with [David] Birney as a reserve. Barlow pushed forward with great vigor, under a heavy fire of both artillery and musketry, through thickets and swamps. Notwithstanding all the resistance of the enemy and the natural obstructions to overcome, he carried a position occupied by the enemy outside their main line where the road makes a deep cut through a bank affording as good a shelter for troops as if it had been made for that purpose. Three pieces of artillery had been captured here, and several hundred prisoners. The guns were immediately turned against the men who had just been using them. No assistance coming to him, he (Barlow) intrenched under fire and continued to hold his place. Gibbon was not so fortunate in his front. He found the ground over which he had to pass cut up with deep ravines, and a morass difficult to cross. But his men struggled on until some of them got up to the very parapet covering the enemy. Gibbon gained ground much nearer the enemy than that which he left, and here he intrenched and held fast.

Wright's corps moving in two lines captured the outer rifle-pits in their front, but accomplished nothing more. Smith's corps also gained the outer rifle-pits in its front. The ground over which this corps (18th) had to move was the most exposed of any over which charges were made. An open plain intervened between the contending forces at this point, which was exposed both to a direct and a cross fire. Smith, however, finding a ravine running towards his front, sufficiently deep to protect men in it from cross fire, and somewhat from a direct fire, put [John] Martindale's division in it, and with [W.T.H.] Brooks supporting him on the left and [Charles] Devens on the right succeeded in gaining the outer – probably picket – rifle-pits. Warren and Burnside also advanced and gained ground – which brought the whole army on one line.

This assault cost us heavily and probably without benefit to compensate: but the enemy was not cheered by the occurrence sufficiently to induce him to take the offensive. In fact, nowhere after the battle of the Wilderness did Lee show any disposition to leave his defences far behind him.

Fighting was substantially over by half-past seven in the morning. At eleven o'clock I started to visit all the corps commanders to see for myself the different positions gained and to get their opinion of the practicability of doing anything more in their respective fronts. . . . I concluded . . . to make no more assaults and . . . directed that all offensive action should cease.

I have always regretted that the last assault at Cold Harbor was ever made. . . . At Cold Harbor no advantage whatever was gained to compensate for the heavy loss we sustained. Indeed, the advantages other than those of relative losses, were on the Confederate side. Before that, the Army of Northern Virginia seemed to have acquired a wholesome regard for the courage, endurance, and soldierly qualities generally of the Army of the Potomac. They no longer wanted to fight them "one Confederate to five Yanks." Indeed, they seemed to have given up any idea of gaining any advantage of their antagonist in the open field. They had come to much prefer breastworks in their front to the Army of the Potomac. This charge seemed to revive their hopes temporarily; but it was of short duration. The effect upon the Army of the Potomac was the reverse. When we reached the James River, however, all effects of the battle of Cold Harbor seemed to have disappeared. . . .

BELOW: An Alfred Waud sketch of a Union battery in action at Cold Harbor.

GRANT'S GREAT CAMPAIGN—STEVENS'S BATTERY AT COLD HARBOR.—From a Sketch by A. R. Waud.

[See Page 410.]

The campaign thus far had been appalling. Between the Battle of the Wilderness and the end of the Battle of Cold Harbor on June 3 the Army of the Potomac had suffered approximately 50,000 casualties, 41 percent of its original strength. Lee's losses had been numerically lower, but they represented an even higher percentage of his strength, 46 percent. Equally important, whereas Grant could count on large reinforcements to make good his losses, Lee could not. In theory, therefore, Grant could have continued this brutal war of attrition with reasonable prospects of ultimate success, but instead he chose to change his strategy.

Once again he slid around Lee's right flank, but this time, rather than immediately pausing to re-engage Lee, he kept going, for his new objective lay well to the south. It was Petersburg, a town close to Richmond, that protected the rail lines on which the Confederate capital depended for its links to the rest of the Confederacy. If Grant could capture Petersburg, Richmond's fate would be sealed.

Lee could easily have thwarted this daring move, for he had the advantage of good interior lines of communications, whereas Grant's men would be obliged to march 50 miles over swampy ground and to cross two unbridged rivers, the Chickahominy and the James, before joining forces with Union General Benjamin Butler's isolated and immobilized command at Bermuda Hundred and swinging west to attack Petersburg. But Grant counted on Lee's not understanding until too late what he, Grant, really had in mind, and in this he was correct: the Southern commander was taken completely by surprise and would lose several vital days in trying to divine his enemy's intentions.

Nevertheless, it was bound to be a near-run thing, wholly dependent on speed, secrecy, deception where possible, and heroic efforts by Grant's corps of engineers. Miraculously, it worked. By mid-June, Grant had crossed the James, linked with Butler, and gained a brief window of opportunity to attack Petersburg before the enemy could respond. Everything now depended on the efficiency and enterprise of Grant's commanders in the field.

OPPOSITE: Engravings made from Waud sketches of Cold Harbor. Inevitably, they lack the spontaneous power of the original drawings.

BELOW: General Benjamin F. Butler (center left), led the small Army of the James in 1864. He was one of the most inept and intemperate of the "political generals" who burdened the Union army.

The advance of the Army of the Potomac reached the James on the 14th June. Preparations were at once commenced for laying the pontoon bridges and crossing the river. As already stated, I had previously ordered General Butler to have two vessels loaded with stone and carried up the river to a point above that occupied by our gunboats, where the channel was narrow, and sunk there so as to obstruct the passage and prevent Confederate gunboats boats from coming down the river. . . .

I then, on the 14th, took a steamer and ran up to Bermuda Hundred to see General Butler for the purpose of directing a movement against Petersburg, while our troops of the Army of the Potomac were crossing.

I had sent General W. F. Smith back from Cold Harbor by the way of White House, thence on steamers to City Point for the purpose of giving General Butler more troops with which to accomplish this result. General Butler was ordered to send Smith with his troops reinforced, as far as that could be conveniently done, from other parts of the Army of the James. He gave Smith about six thousand reinforcements, including some twenty-five hundred cavalry under [August] Kautz, and about thirty-five

hundred colored infantry under [Edward] Hinks.

The distance which Smith had to move to reach the enemy's lines was about six miles, and the Confederate advance line of works was but two miles outside of Petersburg. Smith was to move under cover of night, up close to the enemy's works, and assault as soon as he could after daylight. I believed then, and still believe, that Petersburg could have been easily captured at that time. It only had about 2,500 men in the defences besides some irregular troops, consisting of citizens and employees in the city who took up arms in case of emergency. Smith started as proposed, but his advance encountered a rebel force intrenched between City Point and their lines outside of Petersburg. This position he carried, with some loss to the enemy; but there was so much delay that it was daylight before his troops really got off from there. While there I informed General Butler that Hancock's corps would cross the river and move to Petersburg to support Smith in case the latter was successful, and that I could reinforce there more rapidly than Lee could reinforce from his position.

I returned down the river to where the troops of the Army of the Potomac now were, communicated to General Meade, in writing, the directions I had given to General Butler and directed him (Meade) to cross Hancock's corps over under cover of night, and push them forward in the morning to Petersburg; halting them, however, at a designated point until they could hear from Smith. I also informed General Meade that I had ordered rations from Bermuda Hundred for Hancock's corps, and desired him to issue them speedily, and to lose no more time than was absolutely necessary. The rations did not reach him, however, and Hancock, while he got all his corps over during the night, remained until half-past ten in the hope of receiving them. He then moved without them, and on the road received a note from General W. F. Smith, asking him to come on. This seems to be the first information that General Hancock had received of the fact that he was to go to Petersburg, or that anything particular was expected of him. Otherwise he would have been there by four o'clock in the afternoon.

Smith arrived in front of the enemy's lines early in the forenoon of the 15th, and spent the day until after seven o'clock in the even-

ABOVE: River steamers land supplies at extended wharves built by Union engineers at City Point.

OPPOSITE TOP: Union cavalry stables at City Point.

OPPOSITE BOTTOM: Grant's army crosses the James using the extraordinary 2100-foot-long pontoon bridge that Union engineers built specially for the operation.

121

RIGHT: The 1st U.S. Colored Infantry Regiment. Black troops formed a significant part of Grant's army in 1864.

ABOVE: When Grant's advance units failed in their first effort to take Petersburg in June the element of surprise created by Grant's strategy was lost, and a long siege became inevitable. Here, Union snipers fire at the Petersburg defenses.

ing in reconnoitering what appeared to be empty works. The enemy's line consisted of redans occupying commanding positions, with rifle-pits connecting them. To the east side of Petersburg, from the Appomattox back, there were thirteen of these redans extending a distance of several miles, probably three. If they had been properly manned they could have held out against any force that could have attacked them, at least until reinforcements could have got up from the north of Richmond.

Smith assaulted with the colored troops, and with success. By nine o'clock at night he was in possession of five of these redans and, of course, of the connecting lines of rifle-pits. All of them contained artillery, which fell into our hands. Hancock came up and proposed to take any part assigned to him; and Smith asked him to relieve his men who were in the trenches.

Next morning, the 16th, Hancock himself was in command, and captured another redan. Meade came up in the afternoon and succeeded Hancock, who had to be relieved, temporarily, from the command of his corps on account of the breaking out afresh of the wound he had received at Gettysburg. During the day Meade assaulted and carried one more redan to his right and two to his left. In all this we lost very heavily. The works were not strongly manned, but they all had guns in them which fell into our hands, together with the men who were handling them in the effort to repel these assaults.

Up to this time Beauregard, who had commanded south of Richmond, had received no reinforcements, except [Robert] Hoke's division from Drury's Bluff, which had arrived on the morning of the 16th; though he had urged the authorities very strongly to send them, believing, as he did, that Petersburg would be a valuable prize which we might seek.

During the 17th the fighting was very severe and the losses heavy; and at night our troops occupied about the same position they had occupied in the morning, except that they held a redan which had been captured . . . during the day. During the night, however, Beauregard fell back to the line which had been already selected, and commenced fortifying it. . . .

Colonel [Joshua Lawrence] Chamber-

lain, of the 20th Maine, was wounded on the 18th. He was gallantly leading his brigade at the time, as he had been in the habit of doing in all the engagements in which he had previously been engaged. He had several times been recommended for a brigadier-generalcy for gallant and meritorious conduct. On this occasion, however, I promoted him on the spot, and forwarded a copy of my order to the War Department, asking that my act might be confirmed and Chamberlain's name sent to the Senate for confirmation without any delay. This was done, and at last a gallant and meritorious officer received partial justice at the hands of his government, which he had served so faithfully and so well.

If General Hancock's orders of the 15th had been communicated to him, that officer, with his usual promptness, would undoubtedly have been upon the ground around Petersburg as early as four o'clock in the afternoon of the 15th. The days were long and it would have given him considerable time before night. I do not think there is any doubt that Petersburg itself could have been carried without must loss; or, at least, if protected by inner detached works, that a line could have been established very much in the rear of the one then occupied by the enemy. This would have given us control of both the Weldon and South Side railroads. This would also have saved an immense amount of hard fighting which had to be done from the 15th to the 18th, and would have given us greatly the advantage in the long siege which ensued. . . .

ABOVE: Union Colonel Joshua Lawrence Chamberlain, of the 20th Maine, was wounded in the fighting at Petersburg on June 17. Grant seized the occasion to award this hero of the Battle of Gettysburg an overdue generalcy.

BELOW: A Union battery at Petersburg in June 1864.

Chapter VI

Petersburg and the Shenandoah Valley

Thus the golden opportunity created by Grant's brilliant strategy slipped away. The Army of Northern Virginia soon pulled in behind the Petersburg defenses and fortified them virtually to the point of impregnability. Both sides dug in for a long siege. But at least some Union officers still held hopes of finding a way to break the stalemate quickly.

BELOW: Petersburg, Virginia.

OPPOSITE TOP: The now-famous James River pontoon bridge that brought Grant and his army to Petersburg.

OPPOSITE BOTTOM: Engineers' drawings of typical Rebel defenses at Petersburg.

On the 25th of June General Burnside had commenced running a mine from about the centre of his front under the Confederate works confronting him. He was induced to do this by Colonel [Henry] Pleasants, of the Pennsylvania Volunteers, whose regiment was mostly composed of miners, and who was himself a practical miner. Burnside had submitted the scheme to Meade and myself, and we both approved of it, as a means of keeping the men occupied. His position was very favorable for carrying on this work, but not so favorable for the operations to follow its

completion. The position of the two lines at that point were only about a hundred yards apart with a comparatively deep ravine intervening. In the bottom of this ravine the work commenced. The position was unfavorable in this particular: that the enemy's line at that point was re-entering, so that its front was commanded by their own lines both to the right and left. Then, too, the ground was sloping upward back of the Confederate line for a considerable distance, and it was presumable that the enemy had, at least, a detached work on this highest point. The work progressed, and on the 23rd of July the mine was finished ready for charging; but I had this work of charging deferred until we were ready for it.

On the 17th of July several deserters came in and said that there was great consternation in Richmond, and that Lee was coming out to make an attack upon us – the object being to put us on the defensive so that he might detach troops to go to Georgia where the army Sherman was operating against was said to be in great trouble. I put the army

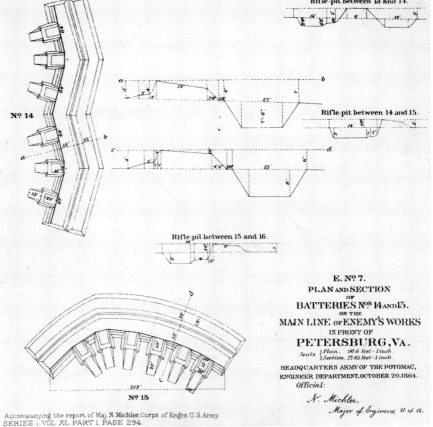

ABOVE: General George Meade. As commander of the Army of the Potomac he was Grant's immediate subordinate during the Virginia campaigns of 1864-65, a trying position for a man as temperamental as Meade. Yet he seems to have handled the assignment capably and, on the whole, rather gracefully.

commanders, Meade and Butler, on the lookout, but the attack was not made.

I concluded, then, a few days later, to do something in the way of offensive movement myself, having in view something of the same object that Lee had had. [Horatio] Wright's and [William] Emory's corps were in Washington, and with this reduction of my force Lee might very readily have spared some troops from the defences to send West. I had other objects in view, however, besides keeping Lee where he was. The mine was constructed and ready to be exploded, and I wanted to take that occasion to carry Petersburg if I could. It was the object, therefore, to get as many of Lee's troops away from the south side of the James River as possible. Accordingly, on the 26th, we commenced a movement with Hancock's corps and Sheridan's cavalry to the north side by the way of Deep Bottom, where Butler had a pontoon bridge laid. The plan, in the main, was to let the cavalry cut loose and, joining with Kautz's cavalry of the Army of the James, get by Lee's lines and destroy as much as they could of the Virginia Central Railroad, while, in the mean time, the infantry was to move out so as to protect their rear and cover their retreat back when they should have got through with their work. We were successful in drawing the enemy's troops to the north side of the

James as I expected. The mine was ordered to be charged, and the morning of the 30th of July was the time fixed for its explosion. I gave Meade minute orders on the 24th directing how I wanted the assault conducted, which orders he amplified into general instructions for the guidance of the troops that were to be engaged.

Meade's instructions, which I, of course, approved most heartily, were all that I can see now was necessary. The only further precaution which he could have taken, and

which he could not foresee, would have been to have different men to execute them.

The gallery to the mine was over five hundred feet long from where it entered the ground to the point where it was under the enemy's works, and with a cross gallery of something over eighty feet running under their lines. Eight chambers had been left, requiring a ton of powder each to charge them. All was ready by the time I had prescribed; and on the 29th Hancock and Sheridan were brought back near the James River with their troops. Under cover of night they started to recross the bridge at Deep Bottom, and to march directly for that part of our lines in front of the mine.

[Gouverneur] Warren was to hold his line of intrenchments with a sufficient number of men and concentrate the balance on the right next to Burnside's corps, while [Edward] Ord, now commanding the 18th corps, temporarily under Meade, was to form in the rear of Burnside to support him when he went in. All were to clear off the

ABOVE: "The Dictator," a huge 13-inch rail-mounted mortar, was one of the most famous siege guns used by the Union at Petersburg.

127

ABOVE: The gabions, trenches, and earthworks used in the construction of the Union's Fort Sedgwick were typical of the passive defenses used by both armies during the siege of Petersburg.

parapets and the *abatis* in their front so as to leave the space as open as possible, and be able to charge the moment the mine had been sprung and Burnside had taken possession. Burnside's corps was not to stop in the crater at all but push on to the top of the hill, supported on the right and left by Ord's and Warren's corps.

Warren and Ord fulfilled their instructions perfectly so far as making ready was concerned. Burnside seemed to have paid no attention whatever to the instructions, and left all the obstruction in his own front for his troops to get over in the best way they could. The four divisions of his corps were commanded by Generals [Robert] Potter, [Orlando] Willcox, [James] Ledlie and [Edward] Ferrero. The last was a colored division; and Burnside selected it to make

the assault. Meade interfered with this. Burnside then took Ledlie's division – a worse selection than the first could have been. In fact, Potter and Willcox were the only division commanders Burnside had who were equal to the occasion. Ledlie besides being otherwise inefficient, proved also to possess disqualification less common among soldiers.

There was some delay about the explosion of the mine so that it did not go off until about five o'clock in the morning. When it did explode it was very successful, making a crater twenty feet deep and something like a hundred feet in length. Instantly one hundred and ten cannon and fifty mortars, which had been placed in the most commanding positions covering the ground to the right and left of where the troops were to

enter the enemy's lines, commenced playing. Ledlie's division marched into the crater immediately on the explosion, but most of the men stopped there in the absence of any one to give directions; their commander having found some safe retreat to get into before they started. There was some delay on the left and right in advancing, but some of the troops did get in and turn to the right and left, carrying the rifle-pits as I expected they would do.

There had been great consternation in Petersburg, as we were well aware, about a rumored mine that we were going to explode. They knew we were mining, and they had failed to cut our mine off by countermining, though Beauregard had taken the precaution to run up a line of intrenchments to the rear of that part of their line fronting

ABOVE: Ambrose E. Burnside, commander of the Union's IX Corps, had to bear ultimate responsibility for the great "mine disaster" of July 30.

LEFT: Edward Ferrero led the (black) division originally assigned to exploit the mine explosion, but for political reasons another division was given the task at the last minute – one of the many errors that produced a fiasco.

where they could see that our men were at work. We had learned through deserters who had come in that the people had very wild rumors about what was going on on our side. They said that we had undermined the whole of Petersburg; that they were resting upon a slumbering volcano and did not know at what moment they might expect an eruption. I somewhat based my calculations upon this state of feeling, and expected that when the mine was exploded the troops to the right and left would flee in all directions, and that our troops, if they moved promptly, could get in and strengthen themselves before the enemy had come to a realization of the true situation. It was just as I expected it would be. We could see the men running without any apparent object except to get away. It was half an hour before musketry firing, to amount to anything, was opened upon our men in the crater. It was an hour before the enemy got artillery up to play upon them; and it was nine o'clock before Lee got up reinforcements from his right to join in expelling our troops.

The effort was a stupendous failure. It cost us about four thousand men, mostly, however, captured; and all due to inefficiency on the part of the corps commander and the incompetency of the division commander who was sent to lead the assault. . . .

By mid-summer it was clear to everyone that the deadlock before Petersburg would not be broken either easily or soon. With their main armies thus frozen into near immobility, both Grant and Lee searched for ways to

BELOW: Reinforced quarters such as this were referred to as "bomb-proof" by the Petersburg besiegers. But it is doubtful that they could have withstood a direct hit by a large-calibre gun.

regain the initiative via maneuver in adjacent areas. Grant had been probing in the Shenandoah Valley since early June, and Lee had countered by sending a 17,000-man corps under Jubal Early into the Valley at midmonth. Early soon brushed aside the feeble Union opposition there, and, since the Valley was now essentially unguarded, Lee ordered Early to move north and make a demonstration against Washington itself. Early was over the Potomac by July 5, and, as Lee had hoped, Washington was in a state of panic and clamoring for Grant to detach forces from Petersburg to come to the city's rescue. Grant, who perfectly understood Early's "raid" for what it was, resisted; and, indeed, by

ABOVE: A U.S. Army blacksmith shapes a shoe for a cavalry mount before Petersburg in August 1864.

LEFT: Confederate General Jubal Early. In June-August Lee, in an effort to divert Grant from Petersburg, had Early make a demonstration against Washington, but Grant was not to be drawn.

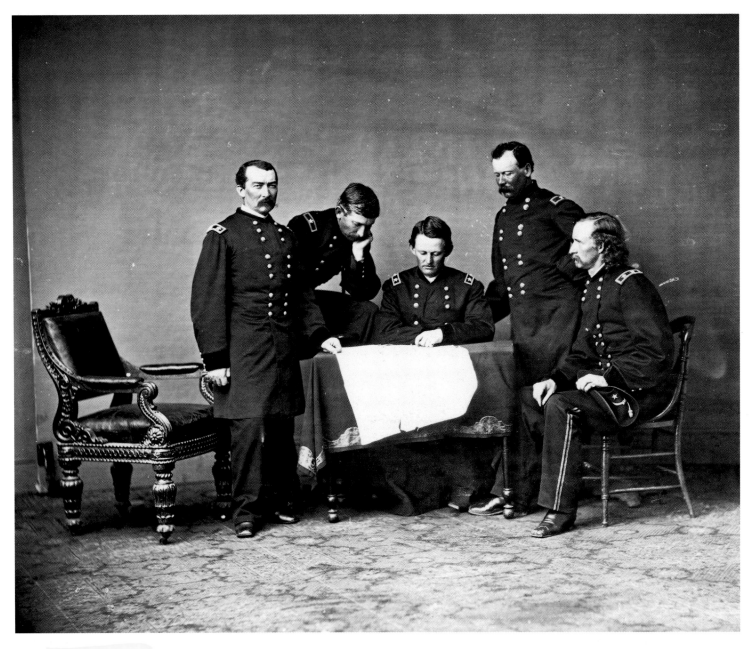

ABOVE: Union cavalry General Philip Sheridan (left) and some of his officers: Wesley Merritt is in the center and George Custer is on the far right. Under Sheridan U.S. cavalry operations for the first time began to surpass those of the Confederates in large-scale effectiveness.

the 12th Early had turned about and was heading back into the Valley.

Grant was not content to let him stay there unmolested. Accordingly, at the beginning of August, Grant created an Army of the Shenandoah and placed it under the command of his premier cavalry general, Philip Sheridan, with orders to clear the Valley once and for all of every vestige of Confederate military presence.

On the 10th of August Sheridan had advanced on Early up the Shenandoah Valley, Early falling back to Strasburg. On the 12th I learned that Lee had sent twenty pieces of artillery, two divisions of infantry and a considerable cavalry force to strengthen Early. It was important that Sheridan should be informed of this, so I sent the information to Washington by telegraph, and

directed a courier to be sent from there to get the message to Sheridan at all hazards, giving him the information. The messenger, an officer of the army, pushed through with great energy and reached Sheridan just in time. The officer went through by way of Snicker's Gap, escorted by some cavalry. He found Sheridan just making his preparations to attack Early in his chosen position. Now, however, he was thrown back on the defensive.

On the 15th of September I started to visit General Sheridan in the Shenandoah Valley. My purpose was to have him attack Early, or drive him out of the valley and destroy that source of supplies for Lee's army. I knew it was impossible for me to get orders through Washington to Sheridan to make a move, because they would be stopped there and such orders as Halleck's caution (and that of the Secretary of War) would suggest would

be given instead, and would, no doubt, be contradictory to mine. I therefore, without stopping at Washington, went directly through to Charlestown, some ten miles above Harper's Ferry, and waited there to see General Sheridan, having sent a courier in advance to inform him where to meet me.

When Sheridan arrived I asked him if he had a map showing the positions of his army and that of the enemy. He at once drew one out of his side pocket, showing all roads and streams, and the camps of the two armies. He said that if he had permission he would move so and so (pointing out how) against the Confederates, and that he could "whip them." Before starting I had drawn up a plan of campaign for Sheridan, which I had brought with me; but, seeing that he was so clear and so positive in his views and so confident of success, I said nothing about this and did not take it out of my pocket. . . .

Sheridan moved at the time he had fixed upon. He met Early at the crossing of Opequon Creek, and won a most decisive victory - one which electrified the country. Early had invited this attack himself by his bad generalship and made the victory easy. He had sent G. T. Anderson's division east of the Blue Ridge before I went to Harper's Ferry; and about the time I arrived there he started

ABOVE: A dramatic example of the growing potency of the Union cavalry would be given in September when Sheridan smashed Early's army at the Battle of Winchester.

LEFT: Edwin McM. Stanton, Lincoln's abrasive but able secretary of war, annoyed Grant by going over Grant's head and interfering with Sheridan's operations in the Shenandoah Valley.

with two other divisions (leaving but two in their camps) to march to Martinsburg for the purpose of destroying the Baltimore and Ohio Railroad at that point. Early here learned that I had been with Sheridan and, supposing there was some movement on foot, started back as soon as he got the information. But his forces were separated and, as I have said, he was very badly defeated. He fell back to Fisher's Hill, Sheridan following.

The valley is narrow at that point, and Early made another stand there, behind works which extended across. But Sheridan turned both his flanks and again sent him speeding up the valley, following in hot pursuit. The pursuit was continued up the valley to Mount Jackson and New Market. Sheridan captured about eleven hundred prisoners and sixteen guns. The houses which he passed all along the route were found to be filled with Early's wounded, and the country swarmed with his deserters. Finally, on the 25th, Early turned from the valley eastward, leaving Sheridan at Harrisonburg in undisputed possession.

Now one of the main objects of the expedition began to be accomplished. Sheridan went to work with his command, gathering in the crops, cattle, and everything in the upper part of the valley required by our troops; and especially taking what might be of use to the enemy. What he could not take away he destroyed, so that the enemy would not be invited to come back there. I congratulated Sheridan upon his recent great victory and had a salute of a hundred guns fired in honor of it, the guns being aimed at the enemy around Petersburg. I also notified the other commanders throughout the country, who also fired salutes in honor of his victory.

I had reason to believe that the administration was a little afraid to have a decisive battle fought at that time, for fear it might go against us and have a bad effect on the November elections. The convention which had met and made its nomination of the Democratic candidate for the presidency had declared the war a failure. Treason was talked as boldly in Chicago at that convention as ever it had been in Charleston. It was a question whether the government would then have had the power to make arrests and punish those who thus talked treason. But this decisive victory was the most effective campaign argument made in the canvass.

Sheridan, in his pursuit, got beyond where they could hear from him in Washington, and the President became very much frightened about him. He was afraid that the hot pursuit had been a little like that of General Cass was said to have been, in one of our Indian wars, when he was an officer of that army. Cass was pursuing the Indians so closely that the first thing he knew he found himself in their front, and the Indians pursuing him. The President was afraid that Sheridan had got on the other side of Early and

LEFT: Philip Sheridan was in many ways typical of the new kind of leadership that emerged in the Union army in the final years of the war. Tough, ruthless, and aggressive, he had an innate sense of command and a keen grasp of tactics. And like Grant and Sherman, he had the flexibility to adapt to the changing nature of war.

ABOVE: Confederate General William Carter Wickham led a brigade in Early's army in the Shenandoah. He resigned in November 1864 to take a seat in the C.S.A. congress.

more use. I approved of his suggestion, and ordered him to send [Horatio] Wright's corps back to the James River. I further directed him to repair the railroad up the Shenandoah Valley towards the advanced position which we would hold with a small force. The troops were to be sent to Washington by the way of Culpeper, in order to watch the east side of the Blue Ridge, and prevent the enemy from getting into the rear of Sheridan while he was still doing his work of destruction.

The valley was so very important, however, to the Confederate army that, contrary to our expectations, they determined to make one more strike, and save it if possible before the supplies should be all destroyed. Reinforcements were sent therefore to Early, and this before any of our troops had been withdrawn. Early prepared to strike Sheridan at Harrisonburg; but the latter had not remained there.

On the 6th of October Sheridan commenced retiring down the valley, taking or destroying all the food and forage and driving the cattle before him, Early following. At Fisher's Hill Sheridan turned his cavalry back on that of Early, which, under the lead of [Thomas] Rosser, was pursuing closely, and routed it most completely, capturing eleven guns and a large number of prisoners. Sheridan lost only about sixty men. His cavalry pursued the enemy back some twenty-five miles. On the 10th of October the march down the valley was again resumed, Early again following.

I now ordered Sheridan to halt, and to improve the opportunity if afforded by the enemy's having been sufficiently weakened, to move back again and cut the James River Canal and Virginia Central Railroad. But this order had to go through Washington where it was intercepted; and when Sheridan received what purported to be a statement of what I wanted him to do it was something entirely different. Halleck informed Sheridan that it was my wish for him to hold a forward position as a base from which to act against Charlottesville and Gordonsville; that he should fortify this position and provision it.

Sheridan objected to this. . . .

Sheridan having been summoned to Washington City, started on the 15th leaving Wright in command. His army was then at Cedar Creek, some twenty miles south of Winchester. The next morning while at Front Royal, Sheridan received a dispatch from

that Early was in behind him. He was afraid that Sheridan was getting so far away that reinforcements would be sent out from Richmond to enable Early to beat him. I replied to the President that I had taken steps to prevent Lee from sending reinforcements to Early, by attacking the former where he was.

On the 28th of September, to retain Lee in his position, I sent Ord with the 18th corps and Birney with the 10th corps to make an advance on Richmond, to threaten it. Ord moved with the left wing up to Chaffin's Bluff; Birney with the 10th corps took a road farther north; while Kautz with the cavalry took the Darby road, still farther to the north. They got across the river by the next morning, and made an effort to surprise the enemy. In that, however, they were unsuccessful. . . .

Sheridan having driven the enemy out of the valley, and taken the productions of the valley so that instead of going there for supplies the enemy would have to bring his provisions with him if he again entered it, recommended a reduction of his own force, the surplus to be sent where it could be of

Wright, saying that a dispatch from Longstreet to Early had been intercepted. It directed the latter to be ready to move and to crush Sheridan as soon as he, Longstreet, arrived. On the receipt of this news Sheridan ordered the cavalry up the valley to join Wright.

On the 18th of October Early was ready to move, and during the night succeeded in getting his troops in the rear of our left flank, which fled precipitately and in great confusion down the valley, losing eighteen pieces of artillery and a thousand or more prisoners. The right under General [George] Getty maintained a firm and steady front, falling back to Middletown where it took a position and made a stand. The cavalry went to the rear, seized the roads leading to Winchester and held them for the use of our troops in falling back, General Wright having ordered a retreat back to that place.

Sheridan having left Washington on the 18th, reached Winchester that night. The following morning he started to join his command. He had scarcely got out of town, when he met his men returning in panic from the front and also heard heavy firing to the south. He immediately ordered the cavalry at Winchester to be deployed across

ABOVE: Like Wickham, James Connor also commanded one of Early's brigades in the Shenandoah. He lost his leg in the fighting there.

LEFT: General John R. Meigs, an engineer on Sheridan's staff, was killed by one of Wickham's scouts. Sheridan, in retaliation, burned all the houses in a five-mile radius of Dayton, Virginia.

the valley to stop the stragglers. Leaving members of his staff to take care of Winchester and the public property there, he set out with a small escort directly for the scene of battle. As he met the fugitives he ordered them to turn back, reminding them that they were going the wrong way. His presence soon restored confidence. Finding themselves worse frightened that hurt the men did halt and turn back. Many of those who had run ten miles got back in time to redeem their reputation as gallant soldiers before night.

When Sheridan got to the front he found Getty and [George Armstrong] Custer still holding their ground firmly between the Confederates and our retreating troops. Everything in the rear was now ordered up. Sheridan at once proceeded to intrench his position; and he awaited an assault from the enemy. This was made with vigor, and was directed principally against Emory's corps, which had sustained the principal loss in the first attack. By one o'clock the attack was repulsed. Early was so badly damaged that he seemed disinclined to make another attack, but went to work to intrench himself with a view to holding the position he had already gained. He thought, no doubt, that Sheridan would be glad enough to leave him unmolested; but in this he was mistaken.

About the middle of the afternoon Sheridan advanced. He sent his cavalry by both flanks, and they penetrated to the enemy's rear. The contest was close for a time, but at length the left of the enemy broke, and disintegration along the whole line soon followed. Early tried to rally his men, but they were followed so closely that they had to give way very quickly every time they attempted to make a stand. Our cavalry, having pushed on and got in the rear of the Confederates, captured twenty-four pieces of artillery, besides retaking what had been lost in the morning. This victory pretty much closed the campaigning in the Valley of Virginia. All the Confederate troops were sent back to Richmond with the exception of one division of infantry and a little cavalry. Wright's corps was ordered back to the Army of the Potomac, and two other divisions were withdrawn from the valley. Early had lost more men in killed, wounded and captured in the valley than Sheridan had commanded from first to last. . . .

OPPOSITE: William W. Averell (seated) was relieved of his brigade command in Sheridan's Shenandoah army for lack of aggressiveness. Such harsh dealing with subordinates was typical of Sheridan.

BELOW: Alfred Waud's sketch of Sheridan's legendary ride at the Battle of Winchester.

Chapter VII

The Union Victorious

OPPOSITE: Fort McAllister, on the Ogeechee River, was the key to Savannah's outer defenses. Sherman took it on his first try on December 13.

RIGHT: Confederate General John Bell Hood.

BELOW: Sherman's men invade South Carolina, February 1865.

After Sheridan's triumph in the Valley serious campaigning in Virginia halted for the winter, but this was not the case in Georgia. On November 16 Sherman pulled the bulk of his army out of Atlanta and set out on his famous (or, to Southerners, infamous) march through Georgia to Savannah and the sea. The Confederate commander, John B. Hood, had hoped to forestall this move by mounting a diversionary offensive behind Sherman in Tennessee, but Sherman was far too good a strategist to be drawn by such a gambit; instead, he merely detached George Thomas to deal with Hood, while he went on about the more important business of cutting the heart of the South in half.

ABOVE: Sherman's men destroy a Confederate railroad. Even before the March from Atlanta to the Sea it was Sherman's deliberate policy to destroy everything that could be of military value to the enemy.

Thomas proceeded on his assignment with such maddening deliberation that the impatient Grant nearly cashiered him. (As we shall see, later on in his Memoirs *Grant tried to make amends for some of the harsh things he had said about Thomas at the time.) But when Thomas finally did strike Hood, on December 15 in the Battle of Nashville, the effect was devastating: thereafter, for all practical purposes Hood's Army of Tennessee no longer existed.*

Sherman occupied Savannah on

December 21, and on February 1, 1865, he embarked on what many historians regard the most brilliant enterprise of his stellar military career, the invasion of the Carolinas. Meanwhile, to the north, Grant was hatching plans for a stroke that he hoped would at last bring the dismal siege of Petersburg to an end. Sheridan, who was essential to the execution of the plan, was temporarily absent, having ridden back into the Shenandoah Valley to mop up what remained of Early's forces, and Grant fretfully awaited his return.

LEFT: The December 15, 1864, Battle of Nashville, in which Union General George Thomas utterly destroyed Hood's Army of Tennessee.

BELOW: Union troops outside Nashville in early December, just before the battle.

ABOVE: A view of Nashville from the roof of the Military College, looking northwest.

Sheridan reached City Point on the 26th day of March. His horses, of course, were jaded and many of them had lost their shoes. A few days of rest were necessary to recuperate the animals and also to have them shod and put in condition for moving. Immediately on General Sheridan's arrival at City Point I prepared his instructions for the move which I had decided upon. The movement was to commence on the 29th of the month.

After reading the instructions I had given him, Sheridan walked out of my tent, and I followed to have some conversation with him by himself – not in the presence of anybody else, even of a member of my staff. In preparing his instructions I contemplated just what took place; that is to say, capturing Five Forks, driving the enemy from Petersburg and Richmond and terminating the contest before separating from the enemy. But the Nation had already become restless and discouraged at the prolongation of the war, and many believed that it would never terminate except by compromise. Knowing that unless my plan proved an entire success it would be interpreted as a disastrous defeat, I provided in these instructions that in a certain event he was to cut loose from the Army of the Potomac and his base of supplies, and living upon the country proceed south by the way of the Danville Rail-

ABOVE: Santa Claus Sherman gives the North a Christmas present in a *Frank Leslie's Illustrated Newspaper* cartoon.

BELOW: Savannah in 1864.

RIGHT: The burden of command is all too evident in this famous informal portrait of an exhausted and careworn Grant at the height of the 1864 campaign.

OPPOSITE: Grant's plan for ending the Petersburg siege in the spring of 1865 was almost wholly dependent on whether Sheridan could turn Lee's flank. "Little Phil" would not let Grant down.

LEFT: Mantleted Union guns before Petersburg.

BELOW: "Bomb-proof" quarters at Union Fort Sedgwick (a.k.a. "Fort Hell") in 1865.

FORT SEDGWICK.

road, or near it, across the Roanoke, get in the rear of Johnston, who was guarding that road, and co-operate with Sherman in destroying Johnston; then with these combined forces to help carry out the instructions which Sherman already had received, to act in co-operation with the armies around Petersburg and Richmond.

I saw that after Sheridan had read his instructions he seemed somewhat disappointed at the idea, possibly, of having to cut loose again from the Army of the Potomac, and place himself between the two main armies of the enemy. I said to him: "General, this portion of your instructions I have put in merely as a blind;" and gave him the reason for doing so. . . . I told him that, as a matter of fact, I intended to close the war right here, with this movement, and that he should go no farther. His face at once brightened up, and slapping his hand on his leg he said: "I am glad to hear it, and we can do it." . . .

Finally the 29th of March came, and fortunately there having been a few days free from rain, the surface of the ground was dry, giving indications that the time had come when we could move. On that date I moved out with all the army available after leaving sufficient force to hold the line about Petersburg. . . . The next day, March 30th, we had

made sufficient progress to the south-west to warrant me in starting Sheridan with his cavalry over by Dinwiddie with instructions to then come up by the road leading north-west to Five Forks, thus menacing the right of Lee's line. . . .

My hope was that Sheridan would be able to carry Five Forks, get on the enemy's right flank and rear, and force them to weaken their centre to protect their right so that an assault in the centre might be successfully made. General Wright's corps had been designated to make this assault, which I intended to order as soon as information reached me of Sheridan's success. He was to move under cover as close to the enemy as he could get. . . .

Sheridan succeeded by the middle of the afternoon [of April 1st] or a little later, in advancing up to the point from which to make his designed assault upon Five Forks itself. He was very impatient to make the assault and have it all over before night, because the ground he occupied would be untenable for him in bivouac during the night. Unless the assault was made and was successful, he would be obliged to return to Dinwiddie Court-House, or even further than that for the night. . . .

It was dusk when our troops under Sheri-

BELOW: Sheridan approaches Five Forks on April 1, 1965. The battle that ensued would mark the beginning of the end of the Civil War.

dan went over the parapets of the enemy. The two armies were mingled together there for a time in such manner that it was almost a question which one was going to demand the surrender of the other. Soon, however, the enemy broke and ran in every direction; some six thousand prisoners, beside artillery and small-arms in large quantities, falling into our hands. The flying troops were pursued in different directions, the cavalry and 5th corps under Sheridan pursuing the larger body which moved north-west.

This pursuit continued until about nine o'clock at night, when Sheridan halted his troops, and knowing the importance to him of the part of the enemy's line which had been captured, returned, sending the 5th corps across Hatcher's Run to just southwest of Petersburg, and facing them toward it. [Wesley] Merritt, with the cavalry, stopped and bivouacked west of Five Forks.

This was the condition which affairs were in on the night of the 1st of April. I then issued orders for an assault by Wright and [John] Parke at four o'clock on the morning of the 2d. I also ordered the 2d corps, General [Andrew] Humphreys, and General Ord with the Army of the James, on the left, to hold themselves in readiness to take any advantage that could be taken from weakening in their front. . . .

I was afraid that Lee would regard the possession of Five Forks as of so much importance that he would make a last desperate effort to retake it, risking everything upon the cast of a single die. It was for this reason that I had ordered the assault to take place at once, as soon as I had received the news of the capture of Five Forks. The corps commanders, however, reported that it was so dark that the men could not see to move, and it would be impossible to make the assault then. But we kept up a continuous artillery fire upon the enemy around the whole line including that north of the James River, until it was light enough to move, which was about a quarter to five in the morning.

BELOW: Victorious Federals pursue fleeing Rebel troops at Five Forks on April 1.

ABOVE: The Kurz & Allison version of the Union victory at Five Forks.

RIGHT: Engineering expert Andrew A. Humphreys served as Meade's chief-of-staff.

FAR RIGHT: Confederate General George Pickett, famous for his charge at Gettysburg, was the loser at the Battle of Five Forks.

At that hour Parke's and Wright's corps moved out as directed, brushed the *abatis* from their front as they advanced under a heavy fire of musketry and artillery, and went without flinching directly on till they mounted the parapets and threw themselves inside of the enemy's line. Parke, who was on the right, swept down to the right and captured a very considerable length of line in that direction, but at that point the outer was so near the inner line which closely enveloped the city of Petersburg that he could make no advance forward and, in fact, had a very serious task to turn the lines which he had captured to the defence of his own troops and to hold them; but he succeeded in this.

Wright swung around to his left and moved to Hatcher's Run, sweeping everything before him. . . .

In the meantime Ord and Humphreys, in obedience to the instructions they had received, had succeeded by daylight, or very early in the morning, in capturing the intrenched picket-lines in their front; and

LEFT: Confederate General John Pegram, who had fought throughout the 1864 campaign, met his death early in 1865 at Hatcher's Run.

BELOW: This segment of the Confederate defensive line at Petersburg is typical of what confronted Union troops when they made their final assault on April 2, 1865.

LEFT: Grant's army had been stalemated behind defensive works such as these outside Petersburg for the best part of a year, yet when Grant finally hit upon a plan to break the siege, it took him only two days to do it.

ABOVE: Union soldiers storm across the parapets of the Petersburg defenses on April 2, 1865. The Confederates withdrew from the city in the night, and Richmond fell the following day.

RIGHT: When they abandoned Richmond, Confederate troops tried to burn their military facilities in the city. The fires got out of hand, and much of the capital of the Confederacy was destroyed.

before Wright got up to that point, Ord had also succeeded in getting inside of the enemy's intrenchments. The second corps soon followed; and the outer works of Petersburg were in the hands of the National troops, never to be wrenched from them again. When Wright reached Hatcher's Run, he sent a regiment to destroy the South Side Railroad just outside of the city. . . .

Lee made frantic efforts to recover at least part of the lost ground. Parke on our right was repeatedly assaulted, but repulsed every effort. Before noon Longstreet was ordered up from the north side of the James River, thus bringing the bulk of Lee's army around to the support of his extreme right. As soon as I learned this I notified [Godfrey] Weitzel and directed him to keep up close to the enemy and to have [G.L.] Hartsuff, commanding the Bermuda Hundred front, to do the same thing, and if they found any break to go in; Hartsuff especially should do so, for this would separate Richmond and Petersburg.

Sheridan, after he had returned to Five Forks, swept down to Petersburg, coming in on our left. This gave us a continuous line from the Appomattox River below the city to the same river above. . . .

The enemy had in addition to their intrenched line close up to Petersburg, two enclosed works outside of it, Fort Gregg and Fort Whitworth. We thought it had now become necessary to carry them by assault. About one o'clock in the day, Fort Gregg was assaulted by [R.S.] Foster's division of the 24th corps (Gibbon's), supported by two brigades from Ord's command. The battle was desperate and the National troops were repulsed several times; but it was finally carried, and immediately the troops in Fort Whitworth evacuated the place. The guns of Fort Gregg were turned upon the retreating enemy, and the commanding officer with some sixty of the men of Fort Whitworth surrendered.

I cannot explain the situation here better than by giving my dispatch to City Point that evening:

BOYDTON ROAD, NEAR PETERSBURG,
April 2, 1865.-4.40 P.M.
COLONEL T. S. BOWERS,
 City Point
 We are now up and have a continuous lines of troops, and in a few hours will be intrenched from the Appomattox below Petersburg to the river above. Heth's and Wilcox's divisions, such part of them as were not captured, were cut off from town, either designedly on their part or because they could not help it. Sheridan with the cavalry and 5th corps is above them. Miles's division, 2d corps, was sent from the White Oak Road to Sutherland Station on the South Side Railroad, where he met

BELOW: An Alfred Waud sketch of a train of railroad cars and a workshop that had been destroyed by Confederates fleeing from Petersburg. The locale is a bridge over the Appomattox River.

ABOVE: The devastation that the Confederate-laid fires caused in Richmond stunned the Union troops who entered the city on April 3. Grant ordered his men to put out the fires, but he did not linger in Richmond. His aim now was to obliterate the Army of Northern Virginia as quickly as possible before it could escape to join with Johnston in North Carolina.

RIGHT: Another dismal scene of gutted Richmond.

them, and at last accounts was engaged with them. Not knowing whether Sheridan would get up in time, General Humphreys was sent with another division from here. The whole captures since the army started out gunning will amount to not less than twelve thousand men, and probably fifty pieces of artillery. I do not know the number of men and guns accurately. . . .

I think the President might come out and pay us a visit tomorrow.

U. S. GRANT,
Lieutenant-General.

During the night of April 2d our line was intrenched from the river above to the river below. I ordered a bombardment to be commenced the next morning at five A.M., to be followed by an assault at six o'clock; but the enemy evacuated Petersburg early in the morning. . . .

The fall of Petersburg doomed Richmond, which was occupied by Union troops the following day. Lee's army, now down to about 35,000 starving men and beginning to disintegrate, fled westward toward Amelia Court House, where Lee hoped to entrain his troops on the Danville Railroad and take them to South Carolina to join forces with Joseph Johnston in his fight against Sherman. But Sheridan cut the Danville line on April 5, and Lee's last hope of escape was gone. What was left of the Army of Northern Virginia struggled on for a few more days, but on April 9, at Appomattox Court House, Lee was finally brought to bay and surrounded by overwhelmingly superior Union forces. It was the end. "There is nothing left for me to do but go and see General Grant," said Lee, "and I would rather die a thousand deaths." A few moments later a Southern rider bearing a white flag galloped towards the Union lines.

BELOW: Union cavalry horses stand tethered to an iron fence amid Richmond's ruins.

When the white flag was put out by Lee, as already described, I was [en route] moving towards Appomattox Court House, and consequently could not be communicated with immediately, and be informed of what Lee had done. Lee, therefore, sent a flag to the rear to advise Meade and one to the front to Sheridan, saying that he had sent a message to me for the purpose of having a meeting to consult about the surrender of his army, and asked for a suspension of hostilities until I could be communicated with. As they had heard nothing of this until the fighting had got to be severe and all going against Lee, both of these commanders hesitated very considerably about suspending hostilities at all. They were afraid it was not in good faith, and we had the Army of Northern Virginia where it could not escape except by some deception. They, however, finally consented to a suspension of hostilities for two hours to give an opportunity of communicating with me in that time, if possible. It was found that, from the route I had taken, they would probably not be able to communicate with me and get an answer back within the time fixed unless the messenger should pass through the rebel lines.

Rebel officers coming into Richmond by the Pontoon bridge to give themselves up.

Lee, therefore, sent an escort with the officer bearing this message through his lines to me.

April 9, 1865

GENERAL:– I received your note of this morning on the picket-line whither I had come to meet you and ascertain definitely what terms were embraced in your proposal of yesterday, with reference to the surrender of this army. I now request an interview in accordance with the offer contained in your letter of yesterday for that purpose.

R. E. LEE, General

LIEUTENANT-GENERAL U. S. GRANT

When the officer reached me I was still suffering with [a] sick headache; but the instant I saw the contents of the note I was cured. I wrote the following note in reply and hastened on:

April 9, 1865.

GENERAL R. E. LEE,

Commanding C. S. Armies

Your note of this date is but this moment (11.50 A.M.) received, in consequence of my having passed from the Richmond and Lynchburg road to the Farmville and Lynchburg road. I am at this writing about four miles west of Walker's Church and will push forward to the front for the purpose of meeting you. Notice sent to me on this road where you wish the interview to take place will meet me.

U. S. GRANT,
Lieutenant-General.

I was conducted at once to where Sheridan was located with his troops drawn up in line of battle facing the Confederate army near by. They were very much excited, and expressed their view that this was all a ruse employed to enable the Confederates to get away. They said they believed that Johnston was marching up from North Carolina now, and Lee was moving to join him; and they would whip the rebels where they now were in five minutes if I would only let them go in. But I had no doubt about the good faith of Lee, and pretty soon was conducted to where he was. I found him at the house of a Mr. McLean, at Appomattox Court House, with Colonel Marshall, one of his staff officers, awaiting my arrival. The head of his column was occupying a hill, on a portion of which was an apple orchard, beyond a little valley which separated it from that on the crest of which Sheridan's forces were drawn up in line of battle to the south. . . .

OPPOSITE TOP: The last C.S.A. general in Richmond, Martin W. Gary, escorted Jefferson Davis to (temporary) safety in South Carolina.

OPPOSITE BOTTOM: Not all the Rebel troops in Richmond fled the city. Some, as shown in this Waud sketch, took the city's fall as an occasion to surrender.

BELOW: The house of Wilmer McLean in Appomattox Court House, Virginia. McLean's former house had been ruined in the Civil War's first big battle, First Bull Run. In this house the war would effectively end.

I had known General Lee in the old army, and had served with him in the Mexican War; but did not suppose, owing to the difference in our age and rank, that he would remember me; while I would more naturally remember him distinctly, because he was the chief of staff of General Scott in the Mexican War.

When I had left camp that morning I had not expected so soon the result that was then taking place, and consequently was in rough garb. I was without a sword, as I usually was when on horseback on the field, and wore a soldier's blouse for a coat, with

the shoulder straps of my rank to indicate to the army who I was. When I went into the house I found General Lee. We greeted each other, and after shaking hands took our seats. I had my staff with me, a good portion of whom were in the room during the whole of the interview.

What General Lee's feelings were I do not know. As he was a man of much dignity, with an impassible face, it was impossible to say whether he felt inwardly glad that the end had finally come, or felt sad over the result, and was too manly to show it. Whatever his feelings, they were entirely concealed

BELOW: Union General Orville Babcock (right) was Grant's aide-de-camp. It was he who was sent to escort General Lee to the surrender talks at the McLean house.

from my observation; but my own feelings, which had been quite jubilant on the receipt of his letter, were sad and depressed. I felt like anything rather than rejoicing at the downfall of a foe who had fought so long and valiantly, and had suffered so much for a cause, though that cause was, I believe, one of the worst for which a people ever fought, and one for which there was the least excuse. I do not question, however, the sincerity of the great mass of those who were opposed to us.

General Lee was dressed in a full uniform which was entirely new, and was wearing a sword of considerable value, very likely the sword which had been presented by the State of Virginia; at all events, it was an entirely different sword from the one that would ordinarily be worn in the field. In my rough traveling suit, the uniform of a private with the straps of a lieutenant-general, I must have contrasted very strangely with a man so handsomely dressed, six feet high and of faultless form. But this was not a matter that I thought of until afterwards.

We soon fell into a conversation about old army times. He remarked that he remembered me very well in the old army; and I told him that as a matter of course I remembered him perfectly, but from the difference in our rank and years (there being about sixteen

years' difference in our ages), I had thought it very likely that I had not attracted his attention sufficiently to be remembered by him after such a long interval. Our conversation grew so pleasant that I almost forgot the object of our meeting. After the conversation had run on in this style for some time, General Lee called my attention to the object of our meeting, and said that he had asked for this interview for the purpose of getting from me the terms I proposed to give his

ABOVE: General Robert Edward Lee, the greatest commander of the Confederacy.

LEFT: A portion of a note from Lee to Grant, part of the historic correspondence between the two commanders regarding Lee's surrender.

161

THE SURRENDER OF GEN. LEE AND HIS ARMY TO LIEUT. GEN. GRANT

HONOR THE ILLUSTRIOUS DEAD,
AND HEARTILY SYMPATHIZE WITH THE SUFFERINGS
OF OUR GALLANT
HEROES AND THEIR FAMILIES.

army. I said that I meant merely that his army should lay down their arms, not to take them up again during the continuance of the war unless duly and properly exchanged. He said that he had so understood my letter.

Then we gradually fell off again into conversation about matters foreign to the subject which had brought us together. This continued for some little time, when General Lee again interrupted the course of the conversation by suggesting that the terms I proposed to give his army ought to be written out. I called to General [Ely] Parker, secretary on my staff, for writing materials, and commenced writing out the following terms:

APPOMATTOX C. H., Va.,
   Apl 9th, 1865.
GEN. R. E. LEE,
   Comd'g C. S. A.
GEN: In accordance with the substance of my letter to you of the 8th inst., I propose to receive the surrender of the Army of N. Va. on the following terms, to wit: Rolls of all the officers and men to be made in duplicate. One copy to be given to an officer designated by me, the other to be retained by such officer or officers as you may designate. The officers to give their individual paroles not to take up arms against the Government of the United States until properly exchanged, and each company or regimental commander sign a like parole for the men of their commands. The arms, artillery and public property to be parked and stacked, and turned over to the officer appointed by me to receive them. This will not embrace the side-arms of the officers, nor their private horses or baggage. This done, each officer and man will be allowed to return to their homes, not to be disturbed by United States authority so long as they observe their paroles and the laws in force where they may reside.
   Very respectfully,
   U. S. GRANT,
   Lt. Gen.

When I put my pen to the paper I did not know the first word that I should make use of in writing the terms. I only knew what was in my mind, and I wished to express it clearly, so that there could be no mistaking it. As I wrote on, the thought occurred to me that the officers had their own private horses and effects, which were important to them, but of no value to us; also that it would be an unnecessary humiliation to call upon them to deliver their side arms.

No conversation, not one word, passed between General Lee and myself, either

ABOVE: The April 9 meeting between Lee and Grant in the McLean house, where the terms upon which Lee surrendered were formally concluded.

OPPOSITE: None of the many artists' versions of Lee's surrender to Grant is fully authentic or even terribly convincing. This one is the work of *Harper's Weekly's* famous Thomas Nast.

RIGHT AND OPPOSITE: Victor and vanquished – Grant and Lee as they looked in 1865. Arguments about who was the better general probably can never be resolved. Both men accomplished things the other did not. Grant never won a battle as dazzling as Lee's famous victory at Chancellorsville; Lee never fought a campaign as brilliant as the one Grant waged against Vicksburg. It is enough to say that both were truly great commanders.

about private property, side arms, or kindred subjects. He appeared to have no objections to the terms first proposed; or if he had a point to make against them he wished to wait until they were in writing to make it. When he read over that part of the terms about side arms, horses and private property of the officers, he remarked, with some feeling, I thought, that this would have a happy effect upon his army.

Then, after a little further conversation, General Lee remarked to me again that their army was organized a little differently from the army of the United States (still maintaining by implication that we were two countries); that in their army the cavalrymen and artillerists owned their own horses; and he asked if he was to understand that the men who so owned their horses were to be permitted to retain them. I told him that as the terms were written they would not; that only the officers were permitted to take their

private property. He then, after reading over the terms a second time, remarked that that was clear.

I then said to him that I thought this would be about the last battle of the war – I sincerely hoped so; and I said further I took it that most of the men in the ranks were small farmers. The whole country had been so raided by the two armies that it was doubtful whether they would be able to put in a crop to carry themselves and their families through the next winter without the aid of the horses they were then riding. The United States did not want them and I would, therefore, instruct the officers I left behind to receive the paroles of his troops to let every man of the Confederate army who claimed to own a horse or mule take the animal to his home. Lee remarked again that this would have a happy effect.

He then sat down and wrote out the following letter:

LEFT: A postwar photograph of leading generals of the Union armies includes: Sheridan (third from left), Grant (eighth from left), Sherman (center, coat over arm).

167

HEADQUARTERS ARMY OF NORTHERN VIRGINIA,
April 9, 1865.
GENERAL:– I received your letter of this date containing the terms of the surrender of the Army of Northern Virginia as proposed by you. As they are substantially the same as those expressed in your letter of the 8th inst., they are accepted. I will proceed to designate the proper officers to carry the stipulations into effect.
R. E. LEE, General
LIEUT.-GENERAL U.S. GRANT

While duplicates of the two letters were being made, the Union generals present were severally presented to General Lee.

The much talked of surrendering of Lee's sword and my handing it back, this and much more that has been said about it is the purest romance. The word sword or side arms was not mentioned by either of us until I wrote it in the terms. There was no premeditation, and it did not occur to me until the moment I wrote it down. If I had happened to omit it, and General Lee had called my attention to it, I should have put it in the terms. . . .

General Lee, after all was completed and before taking his leave, remarked that his army was in a very bad condition for want of food, and that they were without forage; that his men had been living for some days on parched corn exclusively, and that he would have to ask me for rations and forage. I told him "certainly," and asked for how many men he wanted rations. His answer was "about twenty-five thousand:" and I

authorized him to send his own commissary and quartermaster to Appomattox Station, two or three miles away, where he could have, out of the trains we had stopped, all the provisions wanted. As for forage, we had ourselves depended almost entirely upon the country for that.

Generals Gibbon, [Charles] Griffin and Merritt were designated by me to carry into effect the paroling of Lee's troops before they should start for their homes – General Lee leaving Generals Longstreet, [John] Gordon and [William] Pendleton for them to confer with in order to facilitate this work. Lee and I then separated as cordially as we had met, he returning to his own lines, and all went into bivouac . . . at Appomattox.

Soon after Lee's departure I telegraphed to Washington as follows:
HEADQUARTERS APPOMATTOX C. H., Va.,
April 9th, 1865, 4.30 P.M.
HON. E. M. STANTON, Secretary of War, Washington.
General Lee surrendered the Army of Northern Virginia this afternoon on terms proposed by myself. The accompanying additional correspondence will show the conditions fully.
U. S. GRANT,
Lieut.-General.

When news of the surrender first reached our lines our men commenced firing a salute of a hundred guns in honor of the victory. I at once sent word, however, to have it stopped. The Confederates were now our prisoners, and we did not want to exult over their downfall. . . .

GENERAL R.E. LEE'S
FAREWELL ADDRESS

After four years of arduous service, marked by unsurpassed courage and fortitude, the Army of Northern Virginia has been compelled to yield to overwhelming numbers and resources. I need not tell the brave survivors of so many hard-fought battles, who have remained steadfast to the last, that I have consented to this result from no distrust of them; but feeling that valor and devotion could accomplish nothing that would compensate for the loss that must have attended a continuance of the contest, I determined to avoid the useless sacrifice of those whose past services have endeared them to their countrymen. By the terms of agreement officers and men can return to their homes and remain until exchanged. You will take with you the satisfaction that proceeds from the consciousness of duty faithfully performed, and I earnestly pray that a merciful God will extend to you His blessing and protection. With an increasing admiration of your constancy and devotion to your country and a grateful remembrance of your kind and generous consideration of myself, I bid you all an affectionate farewell.

APRIL 10th, 1865.

STRATFORD HOUSE, VIRGINIA, BIRTHPLACE OF LEE.

LEE CHAPEL, VIRGINIA, BENEATH WHICH THE GENERAL WAS BURIED.

RIGHT: Union soldiers pose for a photograph in front of the court house building in Appomattox Court House.

Chapter VIII

Triumph and Tragedy

Lee's surrender effectively ended the Civil War. Five days later the only other important Confederate command left in the field – that of Joseph Johnston, now in North Carolina – asked Sherman for surrender terms, and these were finalized within a week's time.

On April 14, the same day as Johnston's capitulation, Abraham Lincoln asked General and Mrs. Grant to join the President and his wife in attending a play that was to be given that evening at Ford's Theatre in Washington. The Grants regretfully declined on the grounds that they had planned to leave the capital that day to visit their children in New Jersey. The Grants had gotten only as far as Philadelphia when they learned of the President's assassination.

The murder of Lincoln cast a pall over the North's rejoicing, but after a month of mourning the nation's grief was sufficiently purged to permit the observance of at least one solemn tribute to the Union's victorious fighting men. In these closing excerpts from the Memoirs *Grant both describes that impressive ceremony and offers personal impressions of some of the men with whom he served during the war. (It should be noted that the passage relating to General Thomas appears here to be slightly out of sequence.) The final excerpt represents the concluding paragraphs of the* Memoirs.

On the 18th of May orders were issued by the adjutant-general for a grand review by the President and his cabinet of Sherman's and Meade's armies. The review commenced on the 23rd and lasted two days. Meade's army occupied over six hours of the first day in passing the grand stand which had been erected in front of the President's house. Sherman witnessed this review from the grand stand which was occupied by the President and his cabinet. Here he showed his resentment for the cruel and harsh treatment that had unnecessarily been inflicted upon him by the Secretary of War, by refusing to take his extended hand.

Sherman's troops had been in camp on

ABOVE: John Wilkes Booth assassinates Abraham Lincoln in Ford's Theatre on the night of April 14, 1865.

LEFT: Booth leaps from the murdered president's box on to the theater's stage. He broke his leg in the leap but was able to escape from the scene of the crime. He was caught on April 26 and killed in the ensuing shootout.

LEFT: In July 1965 four of the people who were convicted of conspiring with Booth in the assassination plot were hanged. They were Lewis Paine, David Herold, George Atzerodt, and Mary Surratt. The last, Booth's landlady, may well have been innocent.

ABOVE: Lincoln's funeral cortège winds past City Hall in New York City on April 26, 1865. Because Lincoln was a controversial president, the intensity with which the nation grieved his death is all the more extraordinary.

OPPOSITE: On April 21, troops restrain a crowd of grieving Washingtonians from coming too near to the catafalque of the slain president.

the south side of the Potomac. During the night of the 23rd he crossed over and bivouacked not far from the Capitol. Promptly at ten o'clock on the morning of the 24th, his troops commenced to pass in review. Sherman's army made a different appearance from that of the Army of the Potomac. The latter had been operating where they received directly from the North full supplies of food and clothing regularly: the review of this army therefore was the review of a body of 65,000 well-drilled, well-disciplined and orderly soldiers inured to hardship and fit for any duty, but without the experience of gathering their own food and supplies in an enemy's country, and of being ever on the watch. Sherman's army was not so well-dressed as the Army of the Potomac, but their marching could not be excelled; they gave the appearance of men who had been thoroughly drilled to endure hardships, either by long and continuous marches or through exposure to any climate, without the ordinary shelter of a camp. They exhibited also some of the order of march through Georgia where the "sweet potatoes sprung up from the ground" as Sherman's army went marching through. In the rear of a company there would be a cap-

tured horse or mule loaded with small cooking utensils, captured chickens and other food picked up for the use of the men. Negro families who had followed the army would sometimes come along in the rear of the company, with three or four children packed upon a single mule, and the mother leading it.

The sight was varied and grand: nearly all day for two successive days, from the Capitol to the Treasury Building, could be seen a mass of orderly soldiers marching in columns of companies. The National flag was flying from almost every house and store; the windows were filled with spectators; the door-steps and side-walks were crowded with colored people and poor whites who did not succeed in securing better quarters from which to get a view of the grand armies. The city was about as full of strangers who had come to see the sights as it usually is on inauguration day when a new President takes his seat.

It may not be out of place to again allude to President Lincoln and the Secretary of War, Mr. Stanton, who were the great conspicuous figures in the executive branch of the government. There is no great difference of opinion now, in the public mind, as to the

OPPOSITE: One of the most beloved of American icons: Mathew Brady's famed January 8, 1864, portrait of Abraham Lincoln.

BELOW: Lincoln's cabinet in 1863. In the foreground, facing Lincoln, is Secretary of State William Seward, who was badly wounded by Lewis Paine in the execution of the Booth assassination plot.

characteristics of the President. With Mr. Stanton the case is different. They were the very opposite of each other in almost every particular, except that each possessed great ability. Mr. Lincoln gained influence over men by making them feel that it was a pleasure to serve him. He preferred yielding his own wish to gratify others, rather than to insist upon having his own way. It distressed him to disappoint others. In matters of public duty, however, he had what he wished, but in the least offensive way. Mr. Stanton never questioned his own authority to command, unless resisted. He cared nothing for the feeling of others. In fact it seemed to be pleasanter to him to disappoint than to gratify. He felt no hesitation in assuming the functions of the executive, or in acting without advising with him. If his act was not sustained, he would change it – if he saw the matter would be followed up until he did so.

It was generally supposed that these two officials formed the complement of each other. The Secretary was required to prevent the President's being imposed upon. The President was required in the more responsible place of seeing that injustice was not done to others. I do not know that this view of these two men is still entertained by the majority of the people. It is not a correct view, however, in my estimation. Mr. Lincoln did not require a guardian to aid him in the fulfilment of a public trust.

Mr. Lincoln was not timid, and he was willing to trust his generals in making and executing their plans. The Secretary was very timid, and it was impossible for him to avoid interfering with the armies covering the capital when it was sought to defend it by an offensive movement against the army guarding the Confederate capital. He could see our weakness, but he could not see that the enemy was in danger. The enemy would not have been in danger if Mr. Stanton had been in the field. These characteristics of the two officials were clearly shown shortly after Early came so near getting into the capital.

Among the army and corps commanders who served with me during the war between the States, and who attracted much public attention, but of whose ability as soldiers I have not yet given any estimate, are Meade, Hancock, Sedgwick, Burnside, Terry and Hooker. . . . Of those first named, Burnside at one time had command of the Army of the

RIGHT: Union General Ambrose Burnside receives command of the Army of the Potomac in 1862. Burnside had insisted that he was not up to the post, and soon Washington wished it had listened to him.

BELOW: The Union victory at the Battle of the Gettysburg in 1863 made the reputation of George Meade, who took the command of the Army of the Potomac on June 28, three days before the battle.

Potomac, and later of the Army of the Ohio. Hooker also commanded the Army of the Potomac for a short time.

General [George] Meade was an officer of great merit, with drawbacks to his usefulness that were beyond his control. He had been an officer of the engineer corps before the war, and consequently had never served with troops until he was over forty-six years of age. He never had, I believe, a command of less than a brigade. He saw clearly and distinctly the position of the enemy, and the topography of the country in front of his own position. His first idea was to take advantage of the lay of the ground, sometimes without reference to the direction we wanted to move afterwards. He was subordinate to his superiors in rank to the extent that he could execute an order which changed his own plans with the same zeal he would have displayed if the plan had been his own. He was brave and conscientious, and commanded the respect of all who knew him. He was unfortunately of a temper that would get beyond his control, at times, and make him speak to officers of high rank in the most offensive manner. No one saw this fault more plainly than he himself, and no one regretted it more. This made it unpleasant at times, even in battle, for those around him to approach him even with information. In spite of this defect he was a most valuable officer and deserves a high place in the annals of his country.

General [Ambrose] Burnside was an officer who was generally liked and respected. He was not, however, fitted to command an army. No one knew this better than himself. He always admitted his blunders, and extenuated those of officers under him beyond what they were entitled to. It was hardly his fault that he was ever assigned to a separate command.

Of [Joseph] Hooker I saw but little during the war. I had known him very well before, however. Where I did see him, at Chattanooga, his achievement in bringing his command around the point of Lookout Mountain

BELOW: Meade with his staff in 1863. Regarding Meade's notoriously bad temper, one member of his staff wrote, "I don't know any thin old gentleman . . . who, when he is wrathy, exercises less of Christian charity than my well-beloved chief."

and into Chattanooga Valley was brilliant. I nevertheless regarded him as a dangerous man. He was not subordinate to his superiors. He was ambitious to the extent of caring nothing for the rights of others. His disposition was, when engaged in battle, to get detached from the main body of the army and exercise a separate command, gathering to his standard all he could of his juniors.

[Winfield Scott] Hancock stands the most conspicuous figure of all the general officers who did not exercise a separate command. He commanded a corps longer than any

other one, and his name was never mentioned as having committed in battle a blunder for which he was responsible. He was a man of very conspicuous personal appearance. Tall, well-formed and, at the time of which I now write, young and fresh-looking, he presented an appearance that would attract the attention of an army as he passed. His genial disposition made him friends, and his personal courage and his presence with his command in the thickest of the fight won for him the confidence of troops serving under him. No matter how

hard the fight, the 2d corps always felt that their commander was looking after them.

[John] Sedgwick was killed at Spottyslvania before I had an opportunity of forming an estimate of his qualifications as a soldier from personal observation. I had known him in Mexico when both of us were lieutenants, and when our service gave no indication that either of us would ever be equal to the command of a brigade. He stood very high in the army, however, as an officer and a man. He was brave and conscientious. His ambition was not great, and he seemed to

dread responsibility. He was willing to do any amount of battling, but always wanted some one else to direct. He declined the command of the Army of the Potomac once, if not oftener.

General Alfred H. Terry came into the army as a volunteer without a military education. His way was won without political influence up to an important separate command – the expedition against Fort Fisher, in January, 1865. His success there was most brilliant, and won for him the rank of brigadier-general in the regular army and of

LEFT: Joseph Hooker (front, second from right) was to some extent in Coventry when he served under Grant in the Battle of Lookout Mountain. Earlier that year Hooker had led the Army of the Potomac to disaster at the Battle of Chancellorsville, and he had subsequently been eased out of his command of the Army of the Potomac and been given more modest responsibilities. Grant thought Hooker fairly competent militarily, but he disliked and distrusted him. "I . . . regarded him," wrote Grant, "as a dangerous man."

ABOVE: Dapper Winfield Scott Hancock (seated) played a distinguished role in the Battle of Gettysburg and led the Union's II Corps during 1864-65 campaign, in which Grant came to regard him highly. Scott ran for the presidency in 1880, losing by only a narrow margin to James Garfield.

OPPOSITE: A political poster for the 1868 election that would give Grant the first of his two terms in office.

major-general of volunteers. He is a man who makes friends of those under him by his consideration of their wants and their dues. As a commander, he won their confidence by his coolness in action and by his clearness of perception in taking in the situation under which he was placed at any given time. . . .

As my official letters on file in the War Department, as well as my remarks in this book, reflect upon General [George H.] Thomas by dwelling somewhat upon his tardiness, it is due to myself, as well as to him, that I give my estimate of him as a soldier. . . . I had been at West Point with Thomas one year, and had known him later in the old army. He was a man of commanding appearance; slow and deliberate in speech and action, sensible, honest and brave. He

possessed valuable soldierly qualities in an eminent degree. He gained the confidence of all who served under him, and almost their love. This implies a very valuable quality. It is a quality which calls out the most efficient services of the troops serving under the commander possessing it.

Thomas's dispositions were deliberately made, and always good. He could not be driven from a point he was given to hold. He was not as good, however, in pursuit as he was in action. I do not believe that he could ever have conducted Sherman's army from Chattanooga to Atlanta against the defences and the commander guarding that line in 1864. On the other hand, if it had been given him to hold the line which Johnston tried to hold, neither that general nor Sherman, nor any other officer could have done it better.

LEFT: Grant's inauguration in 1869. As president, Grant would display once again the shortcomings that had always before blighted his forays into civilian life. The best that can be said of his two terms in office is that they were honorable failures, in which he was constantly being misled or betrayed by men in whom he had naively put his trust and whom he then defended in a spirit of misplaced loyalty.

BELOW: Grant with his first cabinet. Among those involved in scandals during Grant's administration were Schuyler Colfax, his vice president during his first term, and W.W. Belknap, his second secretary of war.

Thomas was a valuable officer, who richly deserved, as he has received, the plaudits of his countrymen for the part he played in the great tragedy of 1861-5.

* * *

I feel that we are on the eve of a new era, when there is to be great harmony between the Federal and Confederate. I cannot stay to be a living witness to the correctness of this prophecy; but I feel it within me that it is to be so. The universally kind feeling expressed for me at a time when it was supposed that each day would prove my last, seemed to me the beginning of the answer to "Let us have peace."

The expressions of these kindly feelings were not restricted to a section of the country, nor to a division of the people. They came from individual citizens of all nationalities; from all denominations – the Protestant, the Catholic, and the Jew; and from the various societies of the land – scientific, educational, religious, or otherwise. Politics did not enter into the matter at all.

I am not egotist enough to suppose all this significance should be given because I was the object of it. But the war between the States was a very bloody and a very costly war. One side or the other had to yield principles they deemed dearer than life before it could be brought to an end. I commanded the whole of the mighty host engaged on the victorious side. I was, no matter whether deservedly so or not, a representative of that side of the controversy. It is a significant and gratifying fact that Confederates should have joined heartily in this spontaneous move. I hope the good feeling inaugurated may continue to the end.

OPPOSITE: One of the last pictures taken of the Grant family shows them at Mount McGregor, outside Saratoga Springs, in 1885. Grant was already dying of cancer and would not live out the year.

LEFT: Ulysses Simpson Grant, 18th president of the United States and one of history's greatest generals.

Index

Acknowledgments

The publisher would like to thank Design 23, who designed this book, Rita Longabucco, who did the picture research, and Judith Kip, who prepared the index.

All photographs are courtesy of the Library of Congress, except the following:
Anne S. K. Brown Military Collection, Brown University Library: 7, 11, 13, 25(top), 26(top), 27, 42, 57(bottom), 83, 86, 98, 108, 113(top), 118, 180(top).
Brompton Photo Library: 2, 33(top), 39, 41, 42-43, 64, 73(top), 80, 84(bottom), 90(bottom), 99(top), 109(both), 125(bottom), 146, 154(bottom), 161(right), 172.
Chicago Historical Society: 24(left), 40, 94(top).
Historical Society of Pennsylvania: 15.
John Haye Library, Brown University: 178.
National Archives: 4, 8, 12(both), 20-21, 30-31(left, 34, 36, 38(top), 52, 56, 59(right), 69, 72, 75, 88, 92(top), 93(both), 96, 97(both), 99(bottom), 100(top), 116, 119, 120(top), 121, 126-127(right), 128-129(left), 131(top), 132, 151(both), 152-153, 156(bottom), 159, 161(left), 164, 168(top), 179, 181, 186-187.
National Portrait Gallery: 76.
Naval Academy Museum, Courtesy of Beverly R. Robinson Collection: 68(top).
New York Public Library: 49(top).
Norfolk Southern Corporation: 110-111.
Old Courthouse Museum Collection, Vicksburg, MS: 62(top), 82(bottom).
Rutherford B. Hayes Presidential Center: 55(top and right).
US Army Military History Institute, Carlisle, PA: 74(bottom), 107(top), 160.
US Military Academy Archives: 145(top right), 149.
US Naval Historic Center: 140(bottom).
Valentine Museum, Cook Collection: 44(top).
Virginia State Library: 133(top).